NATIONAL CATHOLIC EDUCATIONAL ASSOCIATION

PRESERVING OUR IDEALS:

Papers from the 1993 Principals Academy

National Catholic Principals Academy
July 1993

Back Row: (left to right) Daniel Sherman, Davlyn Duesterhaus, Sr. Mary Frederica Polanski, Patricia Welegala, Sr. Shawn Fitzpatrick, Cynthia Buser, Ellen Manning, Sr. Patricia Ann Czarnota, Sr. Kathleen Heer, Laura Held, Sr. Carol Wiatrek, Sr. Mary Barbara Loch, Sr. Mary Jo Mike, Margaret Sue Jungers, Joseph Sine, Frank Savage; Front Row: Robert Kealey, Margaret Curran, Sr. Christine Kiley, Sandy McGeogh, Sr. Patricia Gavin, Sr. Angela McCarthy, Barbara Coscio, Jeannine Fortunate, Sr. Mary Ann Hart, Sr. St. Fintan Keaveney, Margaret Purcell, Sr. Margaret Langer, Sr. Rosemary Fonck, Patricia Kohl, Mary Helen Thompson, Sr. Regina Haney

Table of Contents

Introduction

"Here was buried Thomas Jefferson, Author of American Independence, of the Statute of Virginia for religious freedom, and the father of the University of Virginia."

Before he died, Thomas Jefferson ordered that the above words be inscribed upon his tombstone. Jefferson wrote these words in order to convey to posterity what he considered to be his most significant accomplishments. Historians might differ with the three achievements that Jefferson chose, perhaps arguing that serving as the third president of the United States or negotiating the Louisiana Purchase might be more important than the documents he authored or an institution he founded. However, Jefferson's act was not a scholarly exercise. It was a personal decision to create a permanent record of the deeds that represented for him the values that he held most dear, the power of the written word, freedom, and intellectual endeavor. With his inscription, Thomas Jefferson enshrined his ideals.

It is fitting, then, that the Jefferson Memorial should be depicted on the cover of the *Papers from the 1993 Principals Academy.* 1993 was the 250th anniversary of Jefferson's birth. When Catholic school principals from around the country met in Washington, DC, the city in which Jefferson served as president, they declared their ideals to the nation. Moreover, they composed articles so that those ideals may be preserved in print.

However, the 1993 Principals Academy was not about the past. It sought to confront the changes that must be made in Catholic education in order to meet the needs of the 1990s and the 21st century. The 1993 Principals Academy embraced the change that is necessary to preserve the ideals of Catholic education.

Many of the challenges and opportunities faced by Catholic education in the 1990s and the 21st Century can be found in the pages of this book. The Principals Academy addressed the topics: Developmentally Appropriate Approaches, Technology, Community Involvement, Catholic Identity, and Diversity. The principals who attended the 1993 Academy benefitted from their networking experiences and from the sharing of ideas with one another. Their purpose here is to share these same ideas with a wider audience so that American Catholic schools will be able to preserve the ideals of the past by meeting the challenges of the future.

Special thanks to Pat Feistritzer for the development of the content treatment, to John Myers-Kearns and Patricia Myers-Kearns for editing, and to Beatriz Ruiz for the design.

Dr. Robert Kealey,
Executive Director, Department of Elementary Schools

Regina Haney, OSF,
Executive Director, National Association of Boards of Catholic Education

Mr. Frank Savage
Executive Director, Department of Chief Administrators of Catholic Education

Section I
Developmentally Appropriate Approaches

Continue the Momentum of Learning

"Every time you tell a child something, you rob him or her of the opportunity to discover it for himself or herself." (Campbell, Early Childhood Education*)*

C hildren seem to come into the world knowing how to learn. By the age of three, they have already mastered a complex language. Research tells us that a child progresses through distinctive stages from the sensori-motor to the formal and is an active learner who interacts with, and adapts to, the environment. The challenge becomes how to continue the momentum.

The aim of schooling, therefore, should be to provide an optimum environment for the child's emerging knowledge when the child is ready to learn specific information. Teaching, then, is a complex task because the nature of the child and his or her learning process are complex. Today's teacher is a facilitator rather than a dispenser of knowledge. He/she provides a curriculum that is nurturing, challenging, exciting, flexible and responds to the developmental needs of the child.

The "average" child simply does not exist. Each child is a unique little package comprised of family background, environment, and some fairly magical factors no one can quite account for.

The concept of Developmental Appropriateness has two dimensions: Age Appropriateness and Individual Appropriateness.

Age Appropriateness. Human development research indicates that there are universal, predictable milestones of growth and change that occur in children during the first nine years of life. These predictable changes occur in all domains of development - physical, emotional, social, and cognitive. Knowledge of typical development of children within the age span served by the program provides a framework from which teachers prepare the learning environment and plan appropriate experiences.

Individual Appropriateness. Each child is a unique person with an individual pattern of timing of growth, as well as individual personality, learning style and family background. Both the curriculum and adults' interactions with the children should be responsive to individual differences. Learning in young children is the result of interaction between the child's thoughts and experiences with materials, ideas and people. When these experiences match the child's developing abilities, while also challenging the child's interest and understanding, learning will take place. *(NAEYC, 1986)*

For example, early learning takes place through the child's senses (touching, tasting, smelling, seeing, and hearing). Children at the early levels should have the opportunity to experiment and learn using as many of the senses as possible. Teachers should prepare the environment for children to learn through active exploration and interaction with adults, other children and materials. Learning activities and materials should be concrete, real, and relevant to the lives of young children. Children need years of play with real objects and events before they are able to understand the meaning of symbols such as letters and numbers. Learning occurs as young children have hands-on experience with objects and interact with people.

Pre-kindergarten and kindergarten

Upon entering a pre-kindergarten or kindergarten classroom, the observer becomes aware of the difference in the physical setting of these rooms from the traditional classroom. One notices the flow of movement within the room from center to center, providing for independent exploration and a variety of stimuli.

The teacher is a facilitator of learning and one that allows the child to participate actively in the growth experience. There is a movement from awareness to exploration, from inquiry to utilization. What teachers do looks different depending upon where individual children are in this cycle of learning.

How children learn

Children actively explore, manipulate, and experiment in an effort to understand their world. This involves everything from tasting and touching, to building and taking apart, from asking and answering questions, to using and merging literary skills. Children construct knowledge, acquire skills and develop dispositions and feelings related to their world.

Play

Play becomes the primary way in which learning occurs in the early years. Play is the best vehicle for integrating learning across all developmental domains: cognitive, language, affective or social, and physical.

In building a pretend tree house, children might negotiate who is to do what job, make written signs to identify their construction, and solve problems related to how to get objects up to the tree house.

Young children also need concrete items for play. A real non-working telephone would be preferred by a younger child, while an older child could substitute one object for another, and create an imaginary toy for play.

There should be a substantial block of time for children to explore and engage in constructive play, such as block building and dramatic play. There needs to be time to invent and play games with rules and to practice newly acquired skills. A sandbox covered with materials can be converted to an art center; while a laundry basket filled with clothes can enhance math skills. An activity in hands-on science such as gardening can provide experience in "weeding, writing and arithmetic." Teachers help enhance children's learning through play by helping children identify their own ideas and putting them into action and by facilitating their problem solving through strategies such as asking questions.

Ages 5 through 8

Age 5 through 8 is a continuum of development from the earlier years. Although the educational format becomes more formalized in organization, and is guided by specific content at the summary level, the learner's needs remain more similar than different to the pre-schooler and kindergartener. An integrated kindergarten through grade three experience best serves the needs of children at this pre-operational stage of development. As such, the methods used to teach the type of content, the kinds of materials, and the physical environment supporting children's learning at this stage should be more similar than dissimilar. If one were to enter a primary classroom today, one would find a greater similarity between this class and the sixth grade class than between the primary and kindergarten. It is simply not supported by what is known about how children at this age learn. (Bredekamp, 1987)

Primary activities

By the age of eight, many of the developmental differences that are apparent in younger children no longer exist in an environment facilitative of the developmental needs of children. (Anastasiow, 1986) (Elkind, 1990) Primary students need to be actively involved in their own learning in order to make connections between what they have learned and what they can do.

In an integrated program unit on seeds, the teacher would begin by asking the students what they know about seeds and what they would like to know. The students would then *explore* with activities on collecting, observing, measuring, classifying, organizing, drawing, graphing and categorizing the seeds.

The teacher would meet with children individually and in small groups, to ask questions on their explorations and to monitor their level of learning. *Questions* would be asked in order to clarify and introduce vocabulary and information and to help students develop concepts. When needed, the teacher would modify and develop additional activities to offer more assistance to the students. The students would be more involved in applying what they learned to new situations through activities, such as writing a booklet, composing a garden song and dramatizing the growth of seeds.

The last stage of this process is *evaluation*, where students would assess their own knowledge, skills, and attitudes. These activities would also include outcomes that a teacher would use to measure a student's progress.

Ages 9 through 11

To continue the momentum of learning in the fourth and fifth grades, mobility, exploration, and experimentation continue to play a role, though perhaps not in the same form or to the same degree, as in the earlier developmental stages. The teacher, while remaining a facilitator, focuses on logical and formal skills.

Teachers are most successful making the transition to more developmentally appropriate activities, when they build on what the students know. An interest survey, given to the students near the beginning of the school year or prior to a particular unit of study could very well provide assistance in this. The following question will assist the teacher in designing activities and developing strategies that will provide for the multiple needs and abilities of the students:

- Do you like to paint, build, write, or read?
- What do you find most interesting (most difficult, most fun) about school?

A checklist for the observer

Using a checklist approach, the observer to the classroom is able to note:

- Is instruction planned to achieve student objectives?
- Is the instruction organized to take into account differences among learners in their capabilities (based on assessment of past performance)?
- Is the instruction organized to take into account differences among learners in their learning styles?
- Is there evidence of different resources used to accommodate more than one learning style to achieve the same objective?
- Are remedial and enrichment activities provided?
- Are options provided that are sensitive to the rates of learning of the students?
- Are the students actively participating in the learning process?
- Is the teacher actively listening and responding to the students?
- Does evaluation provide information on the learning process?
- Is evaluation conducted throughout the lesson? (MTAI, 1992)

No matter what the developmental age, a child's success in the learning process will be better achieved if the momentum of learning is continued from earliest childhood throughout his or her school years. It is therefore critical that the teacher plan for tomorrow and not live in the past. As Henry Adams wrote in 1907, "A teacher affects eternity; he can never tell where his influence stops."

Resources

A Guide to Program Development for Kindergarten: Part I, State of Connecticut Board of Education, 1988.

The Journal of the National Association for the Education of Young Children, NAEYC, 1991.

Mississippi Teacher Assessment Instruments, Office of Teacher Certification, Jackson, MS, January, 1992.

Myths Associated with Developmentally Appropriate Programs, Marjorie J. Kostelnik, *Young Children,* May, 1992.

Developmentally Appropriate Practice in Early Childhood Programs Serving Children from Birth through Age 8, Sue Bredekamp, NAEYC, 1986.

Developmentally Appropriate Teaching in Early Childhood, Early Childhood Series, Dominic J. Gullo, NEA, 1987.

"The Growing Classroom," *Garden Based Science,* Jaffe Montola & Gary Appel, Addison Wesley, 1985.

Sr. Shawn Fitzpatrick
Holy Spirit School
Columbus, Ohio

Mrs. Barbara Ann Coscio
St. Augustine Cathedral School
Bridgeport, Connecticut

Sr. Julia Keaveney
St. Ann's School
Stoughton, Wisconsin

Sr. Mary Jo Mike
Nativity BVM School
Biloxi, Mississippi

The Middle Child in the Catholic School Family: The Needs of Adolescents

Those of us who were teenagers in the sixties thought we were too cool! Our adolescent days brought us sounds of rock and roll and the Beatles, color televison, riding around in red convertible cars, wearing bell-bottom jeans and granny glasses, while sharing a meal around the dinner table with the "whole" family. Today we find our adolescents listening to Heavy Metal CD's, watching MTV music videos in stereophonic sound on television "entertainment centers," wearing designer label clothing, sporting hairstyles in blue-green colors, and playing hours of interactive video games while waiting for their "single parent" head of the household to come home from work. Do you recall having as much exposure to the day-to-day operations of a war as much as children did when they watched TV every day during the Persian Gulf War?

In so many ways, a child experiencing early adolescence in the nineties is nothing like a child growing up in the sixties. Children seem to be growing up a lot sooner than before. Most of us in education continue to ask "Why?" Young people are experiencing more "adult level" behaviors due to the many changes in our societal structure. Who really is the young adolescent of the nineties? How can the Catholic elementary/middle school respond to the "developmentally appropriate" needs of the young adolescent? What kind of support is needed from the Catholic school principal?

What characterizes the young adolescent of the nineties? The young adolescent of the nineties shows marked surges of physical growth, is curious, needs the emotional support of a peer group, and displays a wide range of skills, interests, and abilities unique to his/ her developmental pattern. For the purposes of clarity, we are using the term "young adolescent" to describe children of middle school age, namely, children between the ages of 11 and 14. An adolescent by nature is self-centered, often self-conscious and desires to express his/ her personal opinions. This last trait may often be misconstrued as being argumentative. She/he tends to be intellectually uninhibited and has a strong desire for approval. An adolescent desires to be actively involved in his/her learning processes rather than choosing passive recipiency. Noted psychologist and educator, David Elkind states, "In today's society, we seem unable to accept the fact of adolescence, that there are young people in transition from childhood to adulthood who need adult guidance and direction." (Elkind, 1984)

This transition period calls for a clear understanding of what is "developmentally appropriate" adolescent behavior. Current researchers advocate that developmental behavior must be categorized according to age and individuality. Age appropriate behaviors are often predictable milestones of growth and change that are of the physical, emotional, social, and cognitive nature. Individual appropriate behaviors are unique to the person, and involve the timing of growth, learning styles, and influence of family background.

Interestingly, the Catholic school is the type of school that the Carnegie Council on Adolescent Development (1989) has recommended for middle school age children. In their report, they note that adolescents today are facing far different circumstances than adolescents of previous generations. Today there is less sense of community and less opportunity for close-knit relationships. Under these circumstances, the Carnegie Council Task Force urged that the middle schools:

> ...create small communities of learning where stable, close, mutually respectful relationships with adults and peers are considered fundamental for intellectual development and personal growth. The key elements of these communities are schools-within-schools or houses, students and teachers grouped together as teams, and small group advisories that ensure that every student is known well by at least one adult."

What does the young adolescent need from the Catholic elementary/middle school? She/he needs to be valued and respected as a person while being given opportunities to explore and appreciate his/her own giftedness. She/he desires a greater responsibility in all areas of life. The young adolescent needs to have a feeling of security, to know boundaries and limitations, even though these boundaries will be pushed to the limit. She/he needs to experience a safe and secure environment where She/he can feel free to dialogue about questions concerning values and morals while developing a faith life. An adolescent may often express concerns about his/her future.

How does the Catholic elementary/middle school respond to the needs of the young adolescent? There are three major areas to be considered: adults who work with adolescents, the curricular program, and the overall school environment. Understanding the needs of a young adolescent means that Catholic school principals should seek out and select adults who will listen to the perceptions, interpretations, and concerns of their students and who are willing to negotiate without abdicating appropriate authority. Good middle school teachers recognize and understand the students' needs, interests, backgrounds, motivations, goals, as well as stresses, strains, frustrations, and fears. When teachers use their own wit in ways that don't belittle or bewilder, they may effectively break up tension that otherwise can become disruptive.

The role of the Catholic middle school teacher should be more of a personal guide and facilitator of learning than of a purveyor of knowledge. A respected teacher does not just verbalize what she/he believes; she/he demonstrates personal values in his/her interactions with students. A competent teacher also provides opportunities and guidance to help students become independent learners, those who are able to define their own goals and problems, identify resources, and evaluate outcomes. Today, a good teacher also assists his/her students to become "interdependent" and "cooperative" lifelong learners.

As the twenty-first century approaches, it is evident that the Catholic elementary middle school teacher must prepare the young person to contribute positively to society. The vision of the middle school curriculum should be organized around units whose themes are found at the intersection of early adolescents' concerns about themselves and issues that all of us face in the larger world. Personal, social, technical, and technological skills as well as the development of such concepts as democracy, dignity, and diversity are crucial to the thematic approach of a planned curriculum. The young adolescent must also be challenged to live out Gospel values. David Elkind in his book, *All Grown Up and No Place to Go*, states, "An integrated curriculum of skills, knowledge, and values provides the teenager with a model for constructing an integrated self with specific social skills, social knowlege, and values."

Opportunities for the development of problem-solving skills and reflective thinking processes should be a vital part of curriculum planning. The young person may be defined as a thinking, feeling, and questioning individual. Teachers need to become fully professional guides instead of dull disseminators of information, or as George, Stevenson, Thomason, and Beane state in *Middle School - And Beyond*, "glitzy instructional gymnasts."

All of these components should be part of the Catholic elementary/middle school environment. In our Catholic schools, the atmosphere we seek to create, and which underlies all that we are about, is one of Christian love, respect, service, concern, and nurturing. Any person entering our buildings and classrooms should sense the love and respect present and know that Jesus lives here, by the way people, young and not-so-young, treat one another. The adults who work with middle school children, indeed all of the children, should model a sincere desire to develop their own faith and prayer lives, thus encouraging the young people entrusted to their care to work on their own faith development.

The Catholic elementary/middle school principal is the most important single person in setting the climate and overall attitude of the school. The principal should be a teacher—first, last, and always. The principal works best when she/he relates to and has a sincere personal interest in students. She/he should associate with and be present to students while demonstrating a genuine interest in all facets of student learning. The effective principal is also involved in planning and directing a continuous evaluation of the school program.

An effective principal possesses a clear understanding of the needs of the young adolescent and is capable of translating that understanding into a vision of creating a unique and exciting learning environment. A key component of bringing this vision alive rests in the principal's ability to attract and keep effective teachers. The Catholic elementary middle school needs teachers who are child-centered, willing to participate as team members, are skilled in hands-on approach and serve as visible models of the gospel message. Roland S. Barth, in his book, *Improving Schools From Within*, states, "Principals can orchestrate the school's constellation of unique needs and resources so that everyone gets some of what is needed. And principals have the capacity to stimulate both learning and community."

Our greatest challenge as Catholic elementary/middle school educators is to continue to respond creatively to the ever-changing needs of the young adolescent. Ultimately, our mission is to nurture each child so that she/he recognizes his/her talents and gifts that are God-given. Young adolescents are our leaders of tomorrow. It is a privilege to know that we can help shape the future today.

Resources

Barth, Roland S., *Improving Schools From Within*, Jossey-Bass, San Francisco, CA, 1990.

Elkind, David, *All Grown Up and No Place to Go*, Addison-Wesley, Menlo Park, CA, 1984.

Gatewood, Thomas E. and Dilg, Charles A., *The Middle School We Need*, Association for Supervision and Curriculum Development, Washington, DC, 1975.

George, Paul S., Chris Stevenson, Julia Thomason and James Beane, *The Middle School and Beyond,* Association for Supervision and Curriculum Development, Alexandria, VA, 1992.

Sebring, Penny A. and Camburn, Eric M., *A Profile of Eighth Graders in Catholic Schools,* National Catholic Educational Association, Washington, DC, 1992.

Kathleen Heer
St. Catherine Laboure
Glenview, Illinois

Laura M. Held
St. Philip Neri
Almeda, CA

Extended Care Programs: A Developmentally Appropriate Approach

"**A**w, Mom! Can I please stay a little longer? This is fun!" "Not today. It is after 5:00 p.m., and I need to stop by the store before I fix supper."

Was this child at a pick-up basketball game, the video arcade, the park?

Believe it or not, this was a conversation I overheard between parent and child at our extended-day program at St. Barnabas School in Louisville. We had just begun the program that year and this conversation was a real affirmation for all our planning and work. The students liked the extended program and looked forward to coming.

When we began the program it was enough to be convinced that we were providing a needed service and to be pleased that the children enjoyed the experience of extended-day. Now that the program has tripled in size over a three-year period and has become an extended year (summer care) program, we need to be sure the children are having more than just fun. We need to be sure that the program, which is open to five to twelve-year olds, is meeting individual needs and is developmentally appropriate. It has been my experience that this keeps the children saying, "This is fun."

As principals we are often the directors of these extended-day programs or, even if there is a director, we are the ones who are called if things do not go as they should. Ultimately we must be sure that these extended programs in our schools are of the highest quality. The law supports the establishment of developmentally appropriate programs in order to qualify for licensure. In many states extended school programs are being monitored to be sure that quality child care is available to all children.

Because of the rising concern about the quality of child-care available, the State of Kentucky recently issued emergency regulations governing child-care, including the school-age programs operated at schools. Kentucky law, KRS 199.896 states:

> Such a facility shall provide a planned program of activities geared to the individual needs and developmental levels of the children served. These activities shall provide experiences which promote the individual child's physical, emotional, social and intellectual growth and well-being. The daily program shall provide a variety of creative activities which include art, music, dramatic play, stories, books, science, block building and tactile activities. The program must include a balance of small and large muscle play, quiet and active play, time for free choice of play and sufficient time that children can progress at their own developmental rate.

In light of the increase in the number of Catholic elementary schools offering extended-day programs—30 percent overall, with 50 percent in the southwest and west and 44 percent in inner-city schools (*Momentum,* Sept. 1991) — it would be wise for all of us to know the laws in our state. In a time when liability is a concern, we as administrators can be liable if our programs are not in compliance with civil law.

An outstanding resource for principals on this subject is a 1991 NCEA publication, *Extended Care Programs in Catholic Schools: Some Legal Concerns,* by Sr. Mary Angela Shaughnessy, SCN. Sr. Mary Angela cautions us:

> If the state follows the Kentucky interpretation of extended-day, an administrator who wishes to operate a program as an extension of the school day must insure that there is a structured program that can be substantiated from an educational standpoint. Programs are not required to continue academic instruction for the total session, but there must be a clear academic component such as structured homework time or instruction in sports, music and/or art. What must be avoided is a program that is simply supervised play.

How do we principals determine if our extended-day programs are developmentally appropriate? We need only recall the ideas of Jean Piaget. David Elkind reviews the practical applications of Piaget's philosophy. He reminds us that all learners have developing mental abilities and are assumed to be able to attain these abilities, though not necessarily at the same age. A developmental philosophy sees individual differences in ability as differences in rate of growth. In the developmental philosophy, learning is creative activity. Learners presented with complex problems use complex strategies. As their mental operations develop, children must reconstruct realities. In effect, a child creates and recreates reality out of his or her experiences with the environment. According to Piaget, the aim of education is to facilitate the development of creative activity.

Woolfolk reminds us that kindergarten through sixth-grade children—those attended to most often in the extended-day programs—function in what Piaget calls the concrete operational stage or the stage of "hands-on" thinking. Props and visual aids are essential for learning. Acting out and demonstrating are the best ways to learn. Opportunities for verbalization help children explain what they know. Providing a wide range of experiences helps to build the foundation for learning and language.

Since these extended-day or school-age programs by their names indicate that there is a continuation of the learning process, we must look for activities that actively involve children, and provide opportunities for verbalization and development of large and small motor skills. We must not forget that children not only develop at different rates but that they also have different styles of learning or, as Howard Gardner indicates, different forms of intelligence. In "Different Child, Different Style," Faggella and Horowitz tell us that linguistic learners need books and word-making tools. Logical learners need collections of objects and gadgets to wind up and take apart. Spatial learners like maps and puzzles and to draw and design. Musical learners need tapes and CDs and musical instruments. Kinesthetic learners need physical activity, sports play for large motor development, and manipulatives of all kinds. The interpersonal learner really thrives in the group activities and is often a good group or team leader. The intrapersonal child wants time by himself to "do his own thing." Projects that allow time for individual work or free choice of activities please these children. Our role, then, is to be sure our programs provide different types of materials and a variety of activities.

Child care providers must have the proper background and education to understand the different needs of children at their various developmental stages. Workers whose activities are regulated by the state are usually required to take a certain number of in-service hours each year. At St. Barnabas School our *Handbook for Employees* of the childcare program lists guidelines for working with children at different levels of development. We use the "Developmental Characteristics of School Age Children" compiled by Katherine Abt of the Baltimore City Department of Social Services (1978). This or similar information should be part of any training given to child care workers.

Not only must we be concerned about the materials and activities provided for children (see Appendix A) but it must be clear that extended-day employees understand the emotional needs of children at their different stages. Abt's list of characteristics tell us that six-year-olds respond to affection and warmth but are easily discouraged and wilt under criticism. At this age children cannot tolerate losing. Seven-year-olds want new experiences and like to be given responsibility, but they do dawdle. At this age they are learning to stand up for their rights and are beginning to develop an ethical sense. The eight-year-old is developing a sense of loyalty to friends and joins groups according to sex. At nine a child can be very critical of his own performance and has strong reactions to things he feels are unfair. Ten-year-olds like to be kept busy and are learning to identify personally with heroes. All these children want choices, affection and help with problems and with feelings. To the pre-adolescent the group is very important but so is privacy. They hate to be teased and want independence and security at the same time. Only when child-care providers understand these needs can they really respond to them.

Providing such a comprehensive program is not always easy. In recent conversations with child-care providers at the St. Barnabas and St. Clement Schools in Louisville, the common concern was to meet the needs of the wide range of children who attend extended care. They agreed that the six- to eight-year-olds are easy but the kindergartners and older students are much harder to plan for. Their frustrations are shared by others. The authors of *Who Cares for America's Children?* have this to say about extended programs:

> For 6- to 8-year-olds, many of these programs offer interesting and stimulating activities. For older elementary school children, however, center based models may not be appropriate. Children between the ages of 9-12 clearly need some monitoring and need to know that responsible adults are available to them if needed, but many do not need or want the close supervision that is required. For those who prefer "down time," who need more physical, athletic outlets or who want a quiet place for homework, a child-care center is frequently unappealing.

In my recent conversations with 10- to 11-year-olds from the extended programs mentioned above, I asked them if they liked being there. Their overwhelming response was "yes." When asked why, they preferred this to being home alone, which each identified as the alternative. My personal conclusion is that children need our programs even if they do not always want them.

Recent research of economically disadvantaged children, as reported in *Who Cares for America's Children?* indicates that when an intervention program (quality child-care) is continued into elementary school years, complementing the child's regular school participation, improvement in academic performance can be sustained.

Our programs, if carefully planned, will be able to respond not only to the intellectual needs of children but also to their physical development as well. DeVoe, in his report on the "Activity Patterns of Children During Non-School Hours," finds from children's descriptions of their own activities that most were non-physical in nature, with TV watching being the most common activity. We must carefully assess our programs and be sure that physical activity and gross motor skill development is a part of the daily schedule in every extended-day program.

Who Cares for America's Children? lists a number of agencies who have become the "watchdogs" of child-care operations in this country. These are self-proclaimed child advocates and each has listed guidelines for expectations of quality care by any provider. These are the National Academy of Early Childhood Programs (NAEYC), Washington, DC, the Child Welfare League of America (CWLA), New York, Federal Interagency Day Care Requirements (FIDCR), Washington, DC, and Head Start. We principals need to know how our extended programs comply with these expectations.

By familiarizing ourselves with laws which apply in our state, the developmental philosophy of education and the guidelines mentioned above, it would be obvious upon regular visits to the extended care program whether the physical, emotional and intellectual development of our children is being met. As with our teachers, we must converse regularly with child care providers to determine the responsiveness of these employees to the developmental growth of children.

It is my opinion that the extended-day programs are here to stay and that more and more schools will be adding these programs. Our parents look to them for a safe and convenient environment for their children and can rightfully expect that their children's growth and development will be enhanced in these programs.

Resources

Debusk, Sharon and Leslie, Kathy, "How Can We Help?" *Momentum*, Journal of NCEA, Sept. 1991, Vol. XXII No.3, p.27.

DeVoe, Dale and Mize, Monica, "Activity Patterns of Children During Non-School Hours," *Education*, Vol 13, pp. 322-324.

Elkind, David, "Developmentally Appropriate Practice: Philosophical and Practical Implications," *Phi Delta Kappan*, Oct. 1989.

Faggella, Kathy and Horowitz, Janet, "Different Child, Different Style," *Instructor*, Sept. 1990.

Hayes, Cheryl D., Palmer, John L., and Zaslow, Martha J., Ed., *Who Cares for America's Children? - Child Care Policy for the 1990's.* National Academy Press, Washington, DC, 1990, pp. 170-172.

Johnson, Michael, "Howard Gardner: Redefining Intelligence," *Cardinal Principles*, A Publication of the University of Louisville School of Education, Louisville, KY, 1990.

Shaughnessy, Sr. Mary Angela, SCN, *Extended Care Programs in Catholic Schools: Some Legal Concerns*, National Catholic Educational Association, Washington, DC, 1991.

Woolfolk, Anita E., *Educational Psychology*, Prentice Hall, NJ, 1990, pp. 50-51.

Emergency Regulations on Day Care Operations, Kentucky State Legislature, Frankfort, KY, Spring 1993.

Handbook for Employees, St. Barnabas After School Child Care, Louisville, KY, 1992-93.

Mary Helen Thompson
St. Barnabas School
Louisville, Kentucky

Appendix A:

Extended Care Programs
A Developmentally Appropriate Approach
Checklist for Principals

Check the materials, activities and interactions that you regularly observe as you visit your extended care program. A quality program will be responsive to each child's developmental stage and type of intelligence.

MATERIALS	ACTIVITIES	INTERACTIONS
Linguistic Learner		

Books

Books	Reading___	Adult led games___
Readiness___	Storytelling___	Reading to children___
Young Reader___	Put on plays___	Snack with children___
Chapter books___	Creative writing___	Affection shown___
Multicultural___	Audio/video taping___	Positive praise___
On tape___	Board games___	Review expectations
	Playing school___	regularly___
	Trips to library___	Provide for choices___

Word Making Tool

Paper, pencils, crayons___
Write on board, markers___
Letter stamps___
Word processor___
Tape recorder___
Puppets___
Videos, filmstrips___

Make up rules
   together___
Children take turns as
   leaders___
Opportunities for
   responsibility___
Group discussion of
   consequences___

Logical/Spatial Learner

Hands-On

Flannel board___	Classifying objects___	Participative
Clock___	Number games___	storytelling___
Telephone___	Play store___	Share treasures___
Kitchen gadgets___	Secret codes/riddles___	Discuss feelings about
Play dishes___	Computer games___	events___
Clothing___	Visit museum___	Take pictures/
Magnets___	Art projects___	videos___
Magnifiers___	Crafts___	Learn about famous
Blocks/legos___	Building toys___	people___
Tangrams___	Model building___	Make family trees___
Clay/play dough___		Have question box___
Puzzles___		

MATERIALS	ACTIVITIES	INTERACTIONS

Logical/Spatial Lerner

Hands-On

Maps___
Mazes___
Spyrographs___
Board games___
Dominoes___

Make friendship
   bracelets___
Send cards to the
   elderly or sick___
Role play___

Musical/Kinesthetic Learner

Musical/rhythm
  instruments___
Tape/record
  player___
Tapes/records___
Wood___
Yarn___
Paint/craft items___
Gym set___
Hoola hoops___

Make own
  instruments___
Dance/exercise to
  music___
Provide quiet listening
  space___
Gymnastics___
Draw to music___
Finger paint___

Bring musicians in___
Share musical
  talents___
Outdoor play___
Organized games___
Go to the park___

Interpersonal Learner

Group games___
Casual discussions___
Joke time___
Show and tell___

Intrapersonal Learner

Quiet space___
Collections___
Cards___
Individualized
  games___

Writing___
Stitchery___
Walks___
Quiet time___

Section II
Technology

In Your
Spare Time

Have you ever heard this commercial?
"Now let's face it. Somewhere between the evening news and your favorite TV reruns, you have some free time. Why not learn a foreign language?"

Yeah, sure! *NOT!*

How many of us are even home before the reruns start? How many of us have the time to watch TV? However, the commercial may be right in one area. We need to use our spare time to keep updated on technology, and keeping updated on technology is like learning a foreign language.

How does a principal keep himself/herself updated in the area of technology? First, and most significant, a principal must come to the conclusion that technology in the classroom is critical. We have a tendency to make time for the things we consider important. Once this commitment is made to find the time and make technological knowledge a priority, the rest is just leg work.

So, where does one start? Read, read, read!

Almost every educational magazine has a section on technology. Then there are magazines just for computers and technological instruction. Among the ones that I found most helpful were *Electronic Learning, The Computing Teacher, T.H.E. Journal,* and *Technology and Learning.* Some journals you can get free and some are very inexpensive. If you do not have the money in your budget for these magazines, ask your home and school association to buy them for your faculty.

Next, begin collecting catalogs on computer hardware and software. Make some time to browse through this literature. Many have articles explaining what an LCD panel is or a CD-rom player. Technology articles are everywhere. Even in the in-flight magazines of air lines there are articles about the newest electronic gadget for the workplace. The newest business application will soon become the latest educational technology. Remember that you and your teachers have to be willing to become students again. Just as you plan for other programs, you as principal, have to write in your weekly calendar a time to devote to learning about technology. And don't forget to look at your local bookstore or newspaper stand. There are many books, direct consumer buyer catalogs, and magazines that will give you a wealth of technological knowledge.

If you are really serious about keeping yourself and your staff updated on technology, attend an educational computing conference. I started my search at the National Catholic Educational Association Convention in New Orleans. I attended every session on technology that I could. What was so great about these workshops was that I heard from teachers and principals who were using the technology daily in their own schools. These presenters became the support network that I could call or visit to learn more.

Educational technology conferences happen all over the place. There are state, regional, and national conventions every year. As *Today's Catholic Teacher* magazine reports, "At an educational computing conference, you will find a variety of worthwhile experiences, including workshops and talks by people—teachers like you—who have successfully implemented technology projects in their classes. Many of them will provide handouts, and most will take questions at the end of the session. Take business cards along for swapping and you have an instant networking opportunity." Conventions with which I am familiar are: the National Education Computer Convention and the Regional Consortium of Educational Technology (RCET).

You can find out about these conventions by looking in the educational computer magazines that were mentioned earlier. Or you can talk to other computer teachers, computer user groups, computer stores, and hardware or software representatives. Also, tap into your local public school or local university. The computer or educational technology specialists at these schools are usually knowledgeable and on convention mailing lists. If you have a modem on your computer and subscribe to an electronic bulletin board like CONNECT or Big Sky Telegraph (out of the University of Montana), you can find out about almost any conventions by leaving an open message to all users. If it is out there, someone will leave you a message. The NCEA FORUM on CONNECT has a section just for conferences and workshops. This has great information on video conferences that can help you train and update your faculty.

While at these conventions, do no forget to visit the exhibits. There you will find various hardware and software, as well as kind people to show you how they works. Some exhibitors, like IBM, Apple Computers, and Optical Data, have labs set up so that you can work hands-on with their hardware and software. Pick up everything that is available, such as free catalogs, sample disks, literature, and other freebies. Later you can read this material to help keep you updated. If you have a schedule like mine, your reading time is at a premium.

So, pass out this plethora of information to your faculty to read and ask them to report at your next faculty meeting what new information they discovered.

As I said before, you must make the commitment to find the time if you are going to make technology a priority. This means you get out of the school building and go on the road. Find substitutes, provide release time, and take your teachers to visit other schools that are using technology. At the NCEA convention, Kate Collins, the vice-principal and American history teacher at St. Monica School in Dallas, Texas presented a wonderful demonstration on the use of multimedia for a social studies classroom. Her use of laser disc and CD ROM technology was exciting. Seeing is believing. By taking my sixth and seventh grade teachers to see it first hand, I was able to have someone else do the in-service, as well as the sales pitch for new technology. Those two teachers came back so enthused, that my fifth- and eighth-grade teachers asked for release time to drive four hours to see it also. Do you think I said "No?"

Your next step toward free knowledge is a sales representative. Remember that at the conventions and exhibit hall you were going to collect all those business cards? Now call these delightful people and ask them to come to your school for a demonstration. This is a great way to learn what is new out there in "tech-know-world." If you do not have the name of a representative and you want to know about, let's say, laser disc players and their teaching potential, simply call the company that produces laser discs or laser disc players. Most of these companies have 800 numbers. The courteous folks at these companies can give you the name of your local representative. I called Duwayne Gandy, our local representative from Optical Data, to view their "Windows on Science" program. He flew from Dallas, Texas to present a one hour in-service for my teachers.

By far, the greatest sources of technological knowledge for me were other principals and computer teachers. Cultivate these people and they can provide you with names to call, things to see, places to visit, and literature to read. Two people who are always willing to talk to principals and teachers about learning and technology are: Kathy Rock, a computer teacher in Houston, Texas, with the Christa McAuliffe Institute for Educational Pioneering and Sister Angela Ann Zukowski, Director of the Center for Religious Communication at the University of Dayton. Kathy and Sr. Angela Ann are key members of the New Frontiers for Catholic Schools Program. This unique program is a systematic way to integrate technology into curriculum and school administration. The NCEA has the first two years of the New Frontiers' video teleconferences on video tape called *New Frontiers Back-Pack.* Your school can apply for a grant that will train a team to develop a plan for technology in the classroom. Call or write the NCEA office for more information.

Both IBM and Apple computers have divisions just for educational technology. EduQuest is the name of IBM's educational division. Both companies have people assigned throughout the nation to be consultants to private/parochial schools. I met these people at the NCEA exhibit booths. Martha Rolley, from Apple computers, was very helpful concerning the NCEA Forum through the CONNECT business information network. If you do not know who is assigned to your area, call IBM or Apple directly.

Local universities are another place to learn about technology and education as well as receiving teacher in-service via satellite technology. Many colleges and universities are using technology to teach future teachers. The entry-level teacher is being trained in the use of technology as a teaching tool. Simply call the college of education and begin the search for who is the resident guru of technologies. These multimedia whizzes can't keep a secret. They love to bring more and more people into the technological age. It's like a mission to them. Take advantage of it!

You don't have a satellite dish? How about your archdiocesan offices? Hospitals and other institutions usually have this technology. As a part of their outreach to the community they might let you use their site to receive a satellite signal.

Finally, ask your own students and parents. There are many people in your own school or parish who know a great deal about technology. Just like you cultivated the relationships with computer consultants, cultivate and listen to the "tech-know" whizzes in your backyard. They also become your best source of funding when it is time to spent money.

Like so many other jobs that principals have, you must plan for it to happen if it is going to happen. Now, if you were smart and skipped to the end of this article because you did not have any "spare" time to read it all, here is a summary check list. Happy hunting!

- Talk to other principals, computer teachers, and people who you know are tech-know-whizzes
- Attend educational technology conventions and workshops
- Take time to investigate the exhibits at conventions
- Visit schools using technology; take your faculty with you
- Talk to salespersons including computer sales representatives
- Go to computer stores
- Read educational computing magazines; thumb through catalogs
- Talk to university and college personnel
- Talk to your parents and students

Resources

Coburn, Janet, "Technology for Technophobes," *Today's Catholic Teacher,* Vol. 28, No. 8, May, 1993.

Kathy Rock
8214 Knotty Green Drive
Houston, TX, 77084
(713) 550-6959

Sr. Angela Ann Zukowski
University of Dayton
Center for Religious Telecommunications
300 College Park
Dayton, OH 45469
(513) 229-3126

EduQuest
Internal Zip HO6A1
4111 Northside Parkway
Atlanta, GA 30327

Apple Computer, Inc.
7101 College Blvd.
Suite 910
Overland Park, KS 66210
913-451-0470

Joseph E. Sine
St. Charles Borromeo School
Oklahoma City, Oklahoma

Periodicals and Journals

Cable In the Classroom
A+ Publishing
80 Elm Street
Peterborough, NH 03458

The Computing Teacher
International Society for
Technology in Education (ISTE)
1787 Agate Street
Eugene, OR 97403

Telecommunications
Connect, Inc.
10161 Bubb Road
Cupertino, CA 95014
1-800-262-2638

Optical Data
30 Technology Drive
Warren, NJ 07059
1-800-524-2481

Catalogs
Dell Marketing L.P.
9505 Arboretum Boulevard
Austin, TX 78759
1-800-879-0814

Educational Resources
1550 Executive Drive
Elgin, IL 60123
1-800-624-2926

Electronic Learning
P.O. Box 53797
Boulder, CO 80322

ENHANCE
Quality Computers
20200 E. Mile Road
St. Clair Shores, MI 48080
1-800-777-3642

inCider/A+
P.O. Box 50358
Boulder, CO 80321

Iris, Inc.
P.O. Box 29424
Richmond, VA 23242

*Journal of Computing in
Childhood Education*
Association for the Advancement
of Computing in Education
P.O. Box 2966
Charlottesville, VA 22902

Technology & Learning
Peter Li, Inc.
2451 E. River Road
Dayton, OH 45439

*T.H.E. Journal (Technological
Horizons in Education)*
150 El Camino Real
Suite 112
Tustin, CA 92680

HELPFUL PEOPLE

Duwayne Gandy
Data Optical Corporation
Hurst, TX
1-800-525-9731

Anita Phillips
St. James School
1224 SW. 41st Street
Oklahoma City, OK 73109
(405) 636-6810

Martha Rolley
Apple Core
(913) 451-0470

Sleepless in D.C.: Late-night Ramblings on Space Technology

My father graduated from an all-boys Jesuit high school in the late 1930s. A certain memory of my brothers' and my thumbing through his senior yearbook has stuck with me to this day. It was triggered by a line in a section of faculty quotes. From the picture above it, I would have guessed the grizzled teacher to be an older, veteran member of the staff. What has haunted me off and on is the blatant, racially abusive tone of the comment.

When considering the segregationist nature of the times, it probably shouldn't be so disturbing. But it was then, and is now, so difficult for me to imagine that type of comment ever coming from a member of a staff, let alone being put into print—especially in our system.

Times (hopefully) have changed. Not overnight, not without immense pain and not without mistakes or failures. And the changes have certainly not even been close to complete. But, change has occurred. The July 4, 1993 edition of the *Washington Post* carried a revealing look at our Independence Day and some shocking explanations as to the racially prejudiced roots behind the fight to break from English dominance. A local observer noted that even as recently as ten years ago a story like that would never have made it to press in this capital city. Our feeble efforts at integration, at cultural understanding, sensitivity and inclusion, have worked toward breaking down some of the barriers and have led to change in racial attitudes. I suffered exposure to fewer racist comments than my father did. I hope my children hear even fewer such remarks.

When that same monumental effort of change is talked about in educational speak, it's most often referred to as "restructuring." Deep at the heart of this notion is the belief that the "system itself must be reorganized from top to bottom in order to achieve the kinds of learning and thinking outcomes now seen as necessary for students." But what does that mean for our Catholic schools as we are thrust (willingly or not) into the twenty-first century? How does technology play a role? At what cost?

It may be easier than we think.

Restructuring

Let me say that for us in the Catholic school system to use the word "restructure" is a mistake. Having to restructure would suggest broadscale systemic breakdown—a failure of what is currently in place. That is not our story.

Robert Kealey, in a masterful presentation on the history of Catholic education in the United States given at the 1993 NCEA Principal's Academy, reminds us that even from the beginning, Catholic schools have been called to be that "union of Christian values and secular subjects" that upholds the dignity and freedom of students to strive toward their leadership and their academic potential. This should include everyone, not just the wealthy, bright, or capable. If the stacks of studies completed over the last 20 years concerning Catholic school efficacy are to be believed, we are accomplishing that goal; even to such an extent that our schools have become the sought-after model for the secular system. Conversely, I can't subscribe to the notion of "if it ain't broke, don't fix it." History is strewn with examples of civilizations, organizations and individuals who did not have, or could not execute, the vision to reach a higher destiny. We need to re-assemble, to re-tool...to evolve.

The Darwinian theory of evolution holds with the "survival of the fittest." Either through adaptability of predatory characteristics or defense mechanisms, those organisms which have survived have done so because they have been better adapted to their environment than others. In our own way, our schools cannot stand still counting on the environment to remain the same. As society (read "market") changes and our students/families (read "consumers") demand more from us, we must be in a position to adapt or face extinction. Technology becomes the vehicle effecting the adaptive change from the didactic lecture world of the Print Generations toward the "adventurous teaching," the passion of life inherent to the Audio-Visual Generation of tomorrow.

Proposal from left field

St. Gambrinus School is celebrating its 70th birthday. Enrollment is steadily increasing, the staff and programs are well-respected, and parish and parent support is high. From the outside, everything looks strong, healthy and alive—and to some extent everything is. However, what is becoming increasingly more apparent to those on the inside is that the facilities are woefully inadequate due to deferred maintenance. What's more, despite remarkable success with tuition structuring, parish financial support and funding development strategies have not yet been fruitful enough to keep pace with the rising costs of salaries and benefits. The view on the horizon is hazy.

The power of long range vision can bring it into view, but it's paralyzingly difficult to know where to begin. No school wants to spend limited dollars on hardware solutions that are obsolete before you unpack them. Administrators ask themselves, "Should I invest in this hard drive or wait to be able to afford CD ROM? If we install these monitors in the classrooms will they be compatible with the coming of High Definition Television (HDTV)? If we network our classrooms now, what happens when we have the opportunity to go on line with fiber optics? What is this electronic 'super highway' I keep reading about?"

Suppose a school budget with limited dollars builds on the technology available in the home to support its educational mission?

With increasing employee costs and an aging building, evolution toward that kind of adventurous teaching demands a lot of imagination. The stretch is a little farther but still within our reach. What could such a technological strategy mean for St. Gambrinus? For my school? For your school?

Let's try to think "outside the box."

The plan

Newsweek reports that there are 92 million households in the United States. Nearly all have televisions and phones, and 25 million have personal computers. Barbara Vanderkolk, workplace researcher and sociologist, points out that in 1991 there were 5.5 million home work stations, creating a new breed of American worker: the telecommuter. By 1995, she predicts that number will grow to over 11 million. Before the end of the decade, virtually all homes will be linked by a "super highway" of fiber optic cable and interactive media. This change is being rushed into completion by the nation's communications giants and has been given highest priority by President Clinton's administration. At the time of this writing, a bill is before Congress which would give schools preferential access to this information conduit. This bill stands a good chance of being passed.

Imagine then:

- A school designed around learning pods—multi-aged, developmentally appropriate groupings—where students would really be empowered to become self-directed learners.
- The teacher, as coach, becomes the supporter, a facilitator rather than a lecturer. We've created a constructivist model of a drawing (á la Dewey and Montessori) where students become active participants in both process and outcome.

Still with me?

- Children may not come at the traditional hours. (God knows, we all don't function equally well at 8am—or 3pm!) Such flexibility could be supported by a year-round schedule. As Chester Finn describes, "[instruction] can come about in July as well as March, on Saturday as well as Tuesday, and at 9[p.m.] as well as 9[a.m.]...[We also] need to erase the unrealistic...assumption that all youngsters can learn the same amount during a 180-day school year."

Don't give up on me yet. I'm just getting started.

- Suppose these pod groups then met only on certain days or times when cooperative group work, discussion or direct instruction was necessary. These lessons, and actually the whole instructional plan of each child, would be overseen by a master teacher who has at her fingertips a teaching station linked to that super highway network of information. CDs? You've got'em. HDTV? No problem. Interactive video? Check. Team teaching a lesson with another teacher in say, East Africa? Dial him up. A modem link networking to a resource lab, the administrator's office, the Library of Congress? Without question. A large-screen monitor, overhead projection device, video cam, printer... You get the picture.

- I contend that these teacher stations, complete with all the trimmings, would still amount to a lesser expenditure than huge computer labs, could be updated more regularly at a lower cost, and may actually be more attractive for grants and outside funding than most current proposals on the table. And if not all kids were attending at the same time, maybe the number of stations needed would be fewer than you think.

Now comes the good part!

- All the repetitive, busy work of drill and practice, workbooks and individual homework takes place at home. By virtue of the link-up with the family residence, these master teachers could make accessible a wealth of practice work or home assignments specifically tailored to the individual child. No longer would we be teaching to the masses imprisoned by the constrictions of four walls, but the reality of true individualized instruction could be prescribed for each child - an individual educational plan or IEP if you will. Even if some of this did take place on terminals or other hardware peripherals somewhere on site, these efforts could easily be monitored by a non-certified yet specifically trained teacher assistant, the parateacher of the 21st century. This implementation would free up valuable time during the work day for the master teacher to jointly plan team lessons with colleagues, stay current in subject matter and techniques (including attending curriculum seminars and learning new technology tools) and meet with individual students needing help or encouragement. In other words, they could really become the consummate professionals we hope they will be.

An administrative side note: once the school is linked to the home, the communication potential is unlimited. Think of the savings just in paper by having electronic audio or visual mailboxes established on line for classroom teachers or for the school office. A simple procedure would allow you to leave messages about upcoming events, announcements, policies, homework, etc. for an incoming caller/viewer to access at their leisure! Think of the time that would be freed up for your staff (and you) to be where you can truly do the most good.

Facilities savings could also be realized. As the baby boomlet (and the continuing malaise in public education) translates into more children desiring admittance into our system, flexible scheduling could place fewer students at any one time in a building, meaning less wear and tear, smaller facilities and more efficient and economical maintenance staffs.

As for assessment, the reality of true portfolios and an outcome-based curriculum is naturally complimented by the power of an interactive system such as described. With minimal effort and planning to design the right configuration, record keeping, scoring processes, even samples of work could be stored and evaluated with much more ease and in much less space.

As always the "Yeah, but(s)..."

I don't know any veteran principal who couldn't anticipate at least thirty "yeah, but(s)..." to the schema above; and most parents would add a hundred more. "My teachers won't go for it." "What about the headaches of scheduling?" "Sounds fine, but I work. What are you going to do about my child being out at noon?" "Our families could never afford the cost of the hardware."

There are many questions to answer and major concepts with which to wrestle. That is always the way with choosing a new path. But isn't that also the fun and beauty?

We dream of an educational system where we finally shift emphasis from whole group to small group and individualized instruction. We long for the role of teacher as coach rather than lecturer. We value a classroom where the main focus of instructional efforts does not benefit solely the better students but pays greater attention to the weaker. We encourage our teachers to adopt a model where their students are actively engaged in the process of learning, where there is cooperation rather than competition. We believe in meeting head-on those issues of students with special needs, of how to appropriately assess student progress, of how to recognize the gifts of all styles of learning—visual, verbal, and kinesthetic.

In a span of two hours one morning this spring, I signed for a parcel delivery on a computerized portable clipboard, watched a sales representative print out an adjusted invoice on a revised sale from a lap-top fax machine, and released a sick student to a parent who was able to leave the office because he could do the rest of his work that day at home through a modem link-up. What may sound like the newest of technology is already old hat in the business world. How, then, can we embrace the power of whatever tools may be at our disposal to achieve our important ends?

Of course, there is no one right way. Only many rivulets trickling toward a main stream. We need only jump in for the ride.

Hope

James Mecklenburger predicts the embrace by educators of new technological advancements taking place only when we adopt "technology the term, as analog for technique instead of using the word as analog for device." He adds, "The technology of lecture, of conversation, of quiz we've done so long it's just what we do." When technology is seen as the means and not the process, substantial change can occur. It will be slow, in steps, with problems and failures, but it can and will come. And we should be there, just as we have in the past. In the book *Megatrends* it is suggested that people involved in a change brought on by technology only proceed to the next level when they are comfortable with the preceding technology. We must take what we know, master it, and then go to the next step. Fear of change is normal. We are creatures who find comfort in sameness and order. It takes courage to move into an unknown.

One last offering

As Catholic educators, we should be even swifer to take our small steps than our secular brothers and sisters. We have committed to an even more challenging venture—one beyond purely an academic nature:

a venture of spirit. But do we view technology, as Sr. Angela Ann Zukowski offers, as a "gift working a call or a threat provoking fear?"

Our children today crave tactile, aural, and visual stimulation. If we are to enable our students to enter into a "dialogue" with their culture by empowering them with the skills to critically interact in a positive, life-affirming way, then we must walk with them and feel it with them, not just think it or intellectualize it. We must be the Good News, with passion and conviction, not just preach words from the book. Our continued success demands that we utilize all our resources creatively and in wise stewardship. The evolution of our system—with the aid of technology—will enable the message to continue into the next century and beyond.

My father did not pass on the same prejudices or bigotry that was apparent in his teacher. He recognized the positive from his days of formation, valued it, and moved ahead. "Different" became not better or worse—just different. The challenge we face is to confront the questions of technology and do the same.

Resources

Collins, Allan, "The Role of Computer Technology in Restructuring Schools," *Phi Delta Kappan*, September, 1991.

David, Jane L., "Restructuring and Technology: Partners in Change," *Phi Delta Kappan*, September, 1991.

"Eyes on the Future," *Newsweek*, May 31, 1993, p. 40.

Gardner, Cheri, "The Tool Kit of Technology," *The Power of Our Ideas*, NCEA, 1993, pp. 109-112.

Hofbauer, George, "We Are Called To The Table: A Look At Diversity," *The Power of Our Ideas*, NCEA, 1993, pp. 73-77.

Kealey, Robert, "Catholic Identity," National Catholic Principals Academy, July, 1993.

Lee, Bernard J., "LIMEX: Distance Education in Intentional Learning Communities," *Momentum*, February/March, 1993.

Mecklenburger, James A., "New Frontiers in Catholic Education," University of Dayton/NCEA video, February, 1993.

Naisbett, James, *Megatrends*, referenced by Sr. Angela Ann Zukowski, "Technology," National Catholic Principals Academy, July, 1993.

O'Brien, Donna Marie, OP, "Instructional Technology Is Now," *The Power of Our Ideas*, NCEA 1993, pp. 113-115.

Sheingold, Karen, "Restructuring for Learning With Technology: The Potential For Synergy," *Phi Delta Kappan*, September, 1991.

Technology For Education Act of 1993, U.S. Senate (proposed) May 27, 1993.

Vanderkolk, Barbara, "Infotechnology: Family Friend or Foe?" *Hemispheres*, July, 1993.

Daniel Sherman
St. John School
Seattle, Washington

Schools Yesterday, Today, and into the 21st Century

Educational systems of the 21st century will be drastically different from those of today. The entire system of education, learning and training in the United States is undergoing a fundamental shift to a new philosophy based on mastery. The switch to mastery learning is facilitated by the use of advanced information technology, which can design, manage, and deliver instruction tailored to individual learners. Emerging developments in communications technology and mass media will impact greatly on the school for the 21st century.

Think back to the days when the classroom was isolated from the real world—a quiet sanctuary where administrators saw that teachers taught and students learned the three R's at a leisurely pace. In the fifties and sixties a set of encyclopedias contained an overwhelming amount of knowledge. Today, all the encyclopedias in your school library can fit on a single disk, and that is nothing. Between now and the year 2000, our access to information will double four times over.

Since the early 1980s learning has become much more family-based than school-based. It has also become much more a transgenerational process. Household use of educational products and services has increased steadily for all members of the family, but especially for children. This growing use has been facilitated by the expansion and diffusion of home information learning technology. A majority of United States homes now have digitally integrated computer systems and information storage systems.

The videodisc has added a new dimension to computer-based training by linking the computer to a potentially vast array of audio-video information. This technology also has the potential to increase the realism and flexibility of computer-based training and to make it more interesting. The new linkages of computer and video technology may provide exciting career opportunities for instructional developers.

How will students, teachers, and administrators manage this massive information explosion?

How will technology be integrated into the administration of the school for the 21st century?

The above questions pose a challenge for the students, teachers, and administrators as we move into the 21st century. As Cheri Gardner, a principal at Saint John the Baptist School in Savage, Minnesota, stated, "The challenge is to integrate technology into the curriculum to transform schools into active, vital work and learning environments."

For a look into the future, I had an opportunity to walk through "Classroom 2000: A Room With a View to the Future" when I attended the NCEA Principals Academy in 1993.

> Classroom 2000 is a state-of-the-art presentation-demonstration center located at Anacostia High School in Washington, D.C. It was created as a component of Project ACCORD, an employability skills development program designed to address the basic academic and employability skills of students in the District of Columbia Public Schools (DCPS).

Classroom 2000 offers a range of multimedia and telecommunications capabilities for in-school and out-of-school community planning and outreach. It was created to extend knowledge about how technology can be used to enhance and support teaching and learning.

I was fascinated with the presentation system which delivered various multimedia formats via a touch-screen interface and remote control. As was explained, the large screen accepts all formats including slides, overhead transparencies, videotapes, videodiscs and cable/satellite transmissions. The user can choose to record independently and simultaneously the live action of the presenter as well as any source material that the presenter might use.

Within the room that housed the demonstration tables, workstations were set up, complete with multimedia equipment for interactive videodisc applications as well as for CD-ROM and barcode applications. These group work areas were also connected to the facility's local area network.

After walking through Project ACCORD's Classroom 2000, I must agree with what Roger Coffee writes in his article, "The Managing Principal." He says, "It's a proven fact that school administrators have to be out in front, not only leading but pushing and pulling." Perhaps we can't afford to develop a Classroom 2000 similar to Project ACCORD's but as administrators, we can in-service our teachers through the use of telecommunications, enabling them to interact with other professionals. We can transform our schools into active centers of learning which will be drastically different from schools of yesterday and today.

As Robert Tinker stated in Sister Angela Ann Zukowski's article, "Rethinking Catholic Education: A Dialogue:"

> By 2000, I hope all classrooms will be regularly using computer-to-computer telecommunications for a variety of things—electronic publishing, student projects, teacher networking and bringing new human resources into the classroom through telecommunication conversations.

Resources

Brown, Howard, "Classroom 2000: A Room with a View to the Future," *T.H.E. Journal*, March, 1993.

Gardner, Cheri, "The Tool Kit of Technology," *The Power of Our Ideas, Papers from the 1992 Principals Academy*, p. 112.

Greenfield, Elizabeth, "Administrative Modules: Giving Education a Helping Hand," *T.H.E. Journal*, June, 1993, p. 12.

Schuster, Judy, "The Managing Principal," *Electronic Learning*, May/June, 1993.

Zukowski, Angela Ann, "Rethinking Catholic Education: A Dialogue," *Momentum*, February, 1992, p. 27.

Sister Patricia Ann Czarnota
Saint Titus School
Norristown, Pennsylvania

How Does a Principal Sensitize the Faculty to Use Technology?

S ensitivity sessions are not necessary! This holds true specifically for teacher technology-integration readiness and implementation. The principal can initiate an effective process for implementing technology into the classroom by assessing the needs and concerns of the faculty in a non-threatening manner.

A leadership style that gently facilitates change with a sensitized but visionary process can instill in others the desire to take a risk and to change.

Research testifies to the value of technology in enhancing student learning and achievement. Researchers state, "Only 1/2 of the nation's teachers report ever having used a computer. Only 1/3 have had as little as ten hours training in computer applications. Where technological aids have been made available, however, teachers have been quick to make use of them." One explanation for these statistics may be some pre-conceived ideas teachers have about implementing computers into the classroom. The following statements reflect some typical attitudes.

"I am a people person, machines and I don't work well together."

"I am not mechanical."

"Students work enough on computers at home."

"Students know more than me."

"I am really afraid of computers."

"I've never used them before and don't intend to use them now."

Principals need to assist teachers to learn what they do not know within an environment that does not impose the principal's personal opinion but rather encourages teachers to share hesitations and apprehensions about computer usage. Some tried and true practiced principles for change include the following.

Preparations for change

Construct the reasons for technology change based on research quotes and statistics that support the need for technology in the classroom. Eliciting fears and/or objections through discussion reduces anxieties.

Encourage discussion about the pros and cons of technology use at faculty meetings within a planned time frame.

Set up grade level meetings that concentrate on how professionals can utilize technology in learning centers or work stations. Using video presentations on establishing work stations increases awareness of effective methodologies that coincide with computer implementation. This process can also lead to teacher self-examination of learning modalities and methodologies as applied to technology.

Affirm teachers who are willling to take a risk by demonstrating active participation in computer discussions and workshops. The principal modeling verbal affirmation can increase a teacher's self-confidence as one begins to let go of old ideas and begins to take on new ideas.

Catholic school principals are facilitators of growth and change. As an agent for change, the principal stands side by side with the staff, learning, exploring, working, and implementing. Gentle guidance demonstrates to the teachers the principal's awareness of individual needs, personal readiness, and attitude toward curriculum change and development.

Insuring positive self-esteem and collaborative faculty success in technology implementation can be achieved by developing a plan of action. Through meeting with teachers the principal has established that the input was heard and appreciated and groundwork has been laid for introducing technology into the administrative/classroom curriculum. Assuming that the principal has initiated and solicited monetary assistance from the parent organization and school board the plan begins for technology development.

Technology implementation plan

Initiate a team approach by selecting a resource person to in-service the faculty on user-friendly computers and software. Giving the teachers the opportunity to experiment on a computer in a stress-free environment with colleagues can increase their willingness to take risks. Create an assimilation process for learning by designating teachers to work on age appropriate programs for their teaching grade level.

Explore sending teachers to other schools to observe technology in the classroom setting. This can stimulate the inquiry and Socratic process for motivating teachers toward change. "Technology is being applied in many of our Catholic schools. Classroom teachers frequently are the agents for change, working with colleagues to mold their visions of new and better schools for the 21st century."

Develop teacher ownership and collaborative decision=making by encouraging teachers to select software they feel comfortable implementing. "Focusing on team building, developing collaborative decision-making processes, and exploring new instructional strategies results in richer and more exciting classroom experiences for students."

Selecting a part-time or full-time computer instructor who works with teachers and facilitates the interaction involving teachers and students in the learning environment promotes teacher confidence. This approach promotes a team effort that affects growth and change.

> "Once our students are empowered, through technology, with the ability to wander in the global village, to discover real problems and to interact with others on those problems, they may be reluctant to return to a textbook and a curriculum devoted exclusively to one discipline. If we want a better world for our students, teachers must first show them how to achieve it by working together as a team."

Encourage teachers to increase their teaching potential with stress-reduced training and colleague interaction sessions that enhance ownership for increased technology in the classroom. "As the nation's schools move toward meeting the challenge of educating our children in the 21st century, past methodologies are being reexamined and new approaches explored. Few resources offer more promise and potential for revitalizing the educational process than classroom technology."

The goals of your plan are to increase teacher comfort with computers and educational software which can result in: "Aiding instruction for special needs students, motivating students, improving student attitudes toward learning, encouraging cooperative learning, and stimulating increased teacher/student interaction. Positive changes in the learning environment brought about by technology are more evolutionary than revolutionary. These changes occur over a period of years, as teachers become more experienced with technology."

The principal's challenge is to be sensitive to teachers' anxieties about technology development in the classroom but the principal must lead with a visionary process for technology implementation.

Resources

Avots, Juliette, "Technology as a Bridge," *Educational Leadership,* April, 1993.

Boley, William (principal writer), "Technology and the Thinking Curriculum," *It's Elementary—Elementary Grades Task Force Report,* California Department of Education, 1992.

EduQuest, "Educational Technology Planning Guide for Grades K-8," IBM Educational Systems, Atlanta, GA, 1992.

Gaidimas, Linda, and Susan Walter, "Maines' Common Core of Learning Moves Forward," *Educational Leadership,* May, 1993.

Kachala-Sivin, Jay, and Ellen Bialo, "Report on the Effectiveness of Technology in Schools—1992," New York, 1993.

Ellen Manning
St. Raphael School
Santa Barbara, California

Section III

Community Involvement

Catholic Schools: Prophetic Vision for Parish Life

In ancient times, the prophets encouraged community, kept hope alive within the community, and enabled people to function as faith community—even when the ancient people were sent into exile. As we look forward to the 21st century, American Catholics find themselves exiled from a land of faith and hope. Our world, secular and materialistic, disclaims the existence of God. Twenty-first century American Catholics will depend upon the Catholic schools of tomorrow to be modern day prophets, safeguarding a fragmenting community.

Catholic schools are now and will be in the future entrusted with the Church's mission "to renew the commitment to children and families first by bringing new hope and concrete help." (Putting Children and *Families First*, p.25) In 1972, the American Bishops pastoral letter *To Teach as Jesus Did* encouraged American Catholic schools to share the message, to build community and to enable its students to give service to their fellow human beings. Twenty-one years later, as we prepare to enter the 21st century, Catholic schools are again challenged to provide the form to that vision.

In her educational ministry, the Church is called to proclaim the message revealed by God and manifested in Jesus Christ. Now and in tomorrow's world, Catholic schools need to be prophetic for the local community and others. Administrators and teachers need to be deeply spiritual people, authentically living the Gospel. Nothing less will do; shallow imitations will be unable to satisfy a people dissatisfied by a saturation in materialism.

Authentic prayer must be evidenced in peoples' daily lives. To facilitate this process, Catholic schools must be prayer-filled advocates for children. The school in a fragmented society needs to be the hub of a life-giving support system. In addition to good solid academics, the school can provide:
- a liaison system for parents with social agencies
- flexible time schedules

- basic needs when they are unmet by the family
- early education programs
- parenting programs
- safe havens for children.

When the physical needs of a searching people are met, those who also want more for their children than what a secular society can offer will bring their children to those whose lives bear the fruits of a loving and real relationship with Jesus.

How will schools assist their faculty and staff in developing a genuine spirituality that will empower others to act in prophetic ways? The educational leadership must:

- model Christianity in action as well as word
- provide regular opportunities for prayer and worship experiences
- assist others in sharing their prayer lives
- incorporate regular retreat days into the yearly calendar
- encourage involvement in parish activities
- use outreach gatherings to provide prayer opportunities for parents and children.

People gather together to pray for specific needs and to celebrate their joys and sorrows in a believing community. Catholics need sensitive helpers who will be able to take their hands and lead them to the Father.

With the strength of an inner life, people develop a "liberating self mastery that allows them to commit and serve with an independence and integrity befitting a free people." (Nicgorski, p.7) The love of God proclaimed in the school, through respect and responsibility, must flow into the Christian community. Every person must be viewed as an equally valued member of the organization. (Patterson, p.28) The Spirit must be free to speak through any and all members of the community. Each person must be free to share his or her piece of the wisdom with the community.

Due to the aggressive and individualistic nature of the American society, people need assistance in learning how to openly and freely communicate. Pastors, principals, teachers, parents, and children who interact in this way will assure American society that God will continue to manifest himself within His people as he has promised until the end of time. (Matthew 28:20) This will happen when educational leaders

- engage in consensus decision-making
- support each collective decision
- become good listeners

- involve board members in governance
- help others to seek alternatives to violence through conflict resolution
- model peace-making strategies
- meet regularly with clergy to share goals, ideals, and visions of the parish mission
- respect differences in others
- unite in a commitment to charity and justice
- corporately seek answers to the perceived isolation of economic difficulties.

As citizens of a global community, Catholics need an educational system where their early years are spent in an environment where respect and responsibility are valued, and flow into the community through service.

Catholic schools must continue to encourage others to develop within the hearts of families and children a desire to serve. People naturally enjoy doing for others and can be very creative in their outreach.

Service should be initiated by the school and an on-going part of every family's life. Some ideas for suggested projects are

- simplifying lifestyles (Oxfam America, Fast for a World Harvest)
- addressing injustices (Amnesty International)
- doing little things "to make a difference" (Giraffe Gazette)
- corresponding with children to solve problems (From Kid to Kid, Positive Power)
- teaching people how to analyze and attack social problems (Educating for Citizen Action)
- providing supplies and support to those with AIDS (local coalitions)
- collecting clothing for and feeding the homeless
- writing to prisoners (Kolbe House, Chicago)
- visiting hospitals, nursing homes
- collecting supplies for third world countries

People need to be reminded that service is not just a nice gesture; it is the gospel responsibility of every Christian. People need to be educated to become aware that some of their brothers and sisters are in greater need than others and depend upon others' resources for assistance. With everyone's help, suffering can be alleviated. People, especially children, must be taught a morality of care. (Gorman, p. 43)

Prophecy means being open and allowing God to fashion one in His own pattern, to prophetically speak the message of One so much

His own pattern, to prophetically speak the message of One so much greater. Prophecy presupposes authenticity of the message, sacrifice within community, and courage in service. Catholic educators who are willing to take on this task must ready themselves for the challenge. Educational ministers of the gospel must be truly ready to let go of all selfishness. Their daily witness of selflessness will enable God to penetrate minds, hearts, and souls.

Through message, community, and service God can bring light and life out of a culture influenced by the darkness of materialism and secularism. Everyone must use his or her talents to preserve the gift of Catholic schools in America. Then, parishes will look to the schools to see the reality of their mission being lived!

Resources

Convey, John J., Ph.D., *Catholic Schools in a Changing Society: Past Accomplishments and Future Challenges,* Washington, DC, National Congress, Catholic Schools for the Twenty-First Century, 1991.

Gorman, Margaret, "Catholic Schools: Mirror or Leaven in the Twenty-First Century?" *Momentum,* February/March, 1993, pp. 42-44.

Greeley, Andrew M., "Community as Social Capital: James S. Coleman on Catholic Schools," *America,* September 5, 1987, pp.110-112.

Newman, Fred F., *Educating for Citizen Action,* Berkeley, CA, 1975.

Nicgorski, Walter. "The Moral Crisis: Lessons from the Founding," *The World and I,* September 1987, pp. 7-10.

Patterson, Jerry, *Leadership for Tomorrow's Schools,* Alexandria, VA, ASCD, 1993.

Reck, Carleen, S.S.N.D., *Catholic Identity,* Washington, DC, National Congress on Catholic Schools for the Twenty-First Century, 1991.

U.S. Bishops, *Putting Children and Families First,* Washington, DC, U.S. Catholic Conference, 1991.

Organizations and Further Reading

Fast for a World Harvest
Campaign Connection
Spring, 1987
Oxfam America

Oxfam America
115 Broadway
Boston, MA 02116

Gazette
Giraffe Project
Summer-Fall 1988

Torture in the 80s
Amnesty International/USA
322 Eighth Ave.
New York, NY 10001

_____

Sister Margaret M. Langer
St. Teresa Regional School
Runnemede New Jersey

Patricia M. Welegala
St. Procopius School
Chicago, Illinois

A Small Pebble—A Pool
of Water—Many Waves

As children we have all experienced the wondrous effect of dropping a small pebble into a pool of water and watching the ever widening circles spreading to—imaginings. It could be never ending. Think of where these circles might flow and the influence they might have as they move.

Principals are capable of exerting this kind of influence, but first they must accept the responsibility of being proactive rather than reactive. When hearing news of possible legislative policies that will affect public and private education, they need to seek out information to separate truth from fiction. They need to formulate a plan of action and to initiate the steps that need to be taken.

Brother John McGovern defines public policy as, "A course of action adopted and pursued by the government for the sake of serving the people." This definition does not limit or exclude anyone.

Catholic school principals can do a great deal to gain recognition of the school's rightful place in the field of education. We cannot be afraid to assume the role of leadership and risk-taking or we will lose control.

Every principal needs to know
- education law and Catholic school entitlements—state/federal
- the legislators that represent the city, county, state, and federal governments
- the administrators in the public educational systems: superintendents and principals in the township, county and state
- movers and shakers in the educational field in the area and media contacts.

Armed with this knowledge, principals can accomplish a great deal in securing the rights of Catholic schools. Public school educational officials must recognize that Catholic schools are requesting benefits to create a win/win situation for all children. These children will all come together as future citizens in society.

Much public relations work needs to be done. To develop a vision, it must be supported by others. We are aware of the academic accomplishments of Catholic schools. We are also informed that Catholic schools are more cost-efficient per pupil than public schools. This cost effectiveness and the academic accomplishments of Catholic schools indicate that money alone does not guarantee a school's success.

What makes the difference?

Using the analogy of the pebble and the pool of water, let us follow the flow of the circles.

Resounding waves: the first circle—teachers

In my school, teachers believe in Jesus' command to go forth and teach and that the ripple effect will eventually carry their teachings to all nations. They are informed and willing to attend development seminars to enhance the current curricula. Like all Catholic teachers, they are underpaid and overworked, but keep abreast of public issues that affect their teaching. They are perhaps more influential than the principal in getting parents attuned to public policy. The teachers have carried back to the classrooms experiences from Mr. Wizard, colonial studies in Virginia, whole language seminars and math practicals. They return from these studies renewed, refreshed and enthused. The students learn with new zest. They carry this appreciation to the parents, who in turn praise and inform those who will listen about the accomplishments of the students of St. Paul School.

The second circle—parents

Students carry the "Good News" in Catholic education to the parents. Parents must be involved with educators. They too must accept the vision and support the dream. Catholic education cannot remain a viable alternative without parental involvement. The parents must be the force to carry the message to the public school officials that Catholic school students deserve and are entitled by law to certain rights, namely

- free or reduced lunches
- free or reduced textbooks
- transportation to and from school
- special education services and the transporting of students off-site to and from supportive facilities
- other off-site health services
- special monies from Chapter I and II; Substance Abuse and Violence Prevention; Eisenhower Math/Science, others listed in the *Handbook of Federal Programs Available for Use by Private Schools*

St. Paul School has been fortunate in its relationship with the requested. The principal must be knowledgeable of the law for all children and through meetings with public school officials productive communications are accomplished. Much good press comes with cooperation and good working relationships. Most of the St. Paul students will feed into the public high school. It is a point of pride that we send to the public schools students that are academically and morally prepared to become achievers and leaders in their school. It is a benefit to these schools. Parents must attest to the fact that entitlements and services for Catholic schools will eventually be beneficial to public schools in the community. When they assume ownership of the vision, parents are the most effective force for a writing campaign to newspapers and legislators.

The third circle—city

Along with the normal programs for deterrence to involvement with the law, St. Paul works with a program called Project LEAD - Legal Education And Delinquency. This program is sponsored by Purdue University Calumet. Over a period of ten weeks, various city officials, city and county police, and chain store managers speak to fifth grade students from St. Paul. They are apprised of the law and allowed to tour city offices and the jail. This experience culminates with their written impressions of the experience.

The Fire Chief and local fire fighters certify our seventh and eighth grade students in CPR and the Heimlich maneuver. They bring their equipment for training and testing into the building.

Libraries and book stores approve of our summer reading programs, and set aside suggested books for the students of the school.

The City Park Board recognizes our athletic program by training and certifying coaches and referees for the various sports activities sponsored by the school.

The forth circle—state

The Indiana Non-Public Education Association (INPEA) appears to be the organization through which many direct issues are addressed. Principals are encouraged to become members and to be involved. At meetings public policies are addressed. Three years ago members heard of two new sources of possible monetary support for Catholic schools. This revenue would be forthcoming from public corporation groups: the Golden Rule and COMMIT - Building a Coalition to Make Indiana Schools Better. These corporation groups would reward achieving schools for the improved performance of students. (Since that time it has been reevaluated, and the support for non-public schools withdrawn. COMMIT'S 1993-94 statements support school choice only in reference to public schools.)

57

The fifth circle—nation

The national support ripple is far from the center. However, the distance should not be discouraging. Once again we should use resources that have worked in the past. Be informed, spread the news, encourage parents to be proactive and above all dare to dream, share the vision, and *make waves.*

Resources

Doyle, Michelle, *Handbook of Federal Programs*, available through the Department of Private School Education, Washington, DC.

Knarr, Mary, fifth grade teacher, St. Paul School, Valparaiso, IN.

McGovern, John, NCEA Catholic Schools Public Policy Councils, Washington, DC.

Patricia A. Kohl
St. Paul School
Valparaiso, Indiana

The Role of the Principal in Giving Ownership to the Board

"The willingness to adjust yesterday's truths in light of today's discoveries" is one of the hallmarks of sucessful leaders. (Indrisano, 1989) In selecting from the many options available to them, most principals choose courses of action which they believe will be successful. (Smith, 1989) Catholic school principals, characterized throughout the years by their dedication to excellence, must seriously examine the concept of shared governance if they are to continue as sucessful leaders while moving their schools into the 21st century.

A limited beginning

In the 19th century, lay boards of trustees were common within Catholic church structures. Since some states denied the right of the Church to hold property, lay trustees were often designated to hold Church property in their own names. This relationship, which arose out of necessity and not from a conviction of the need to share authority and ownership with the people of God, gave rise to some difficulty "in which lay officers at times became defiant of the authority of the heirarchy," and other situations which were perceived to "hinder the progress of schools." (Buetow, 1985)

Boards and councils of education were called by the Councils of Baltimore in the late 1800s, (Sheehan, 1990) but authority and governance continued to reside primarily with bishops, pastors, and professionals.

A strengthened present

After Vatican II, there was renewed interest in Catholic school boards. Many involved in Catholic education agreed with the documents which stated that parents were the first and foremost educators of their children and were encouraged by the Council's call for more involvement by the laity in the life of the Church. School boards were seen as excellent vehicles through which Church leaders could share responsibility and encourage parents to participate in decision making. Many Catholic schools in the United States have some form of shared governance structure. Statistics are not available, however, on how many boards are truly effective or how many board members feel that they posess ownership of and responsibility for the mission of the school.

For school boards to be effective, Catholic school principals must be convinced that sharing the governance of "their" schools is one of the most effective ways of continually improving them. School boards, they must realize, are not something merely imposed on them by diocesan regulations or *pro forma* groups with whom to meet each month in order to get rubber-stamp approval for plans. They are, instead, facilitators of progress and allies in improvement. Research has shown that

"Boards run in the most successful schools of quality build strong linkages with major stockholders, recognizing them as essential contributors to schools' ongoing improvement processes." (Bonstingl, 1992, p. 41)

Once Catholic school principals are convinced of the need for shared governance, they must take steps to ensure that their board is comprised of people willing to meet the challenge of carrying our schools into the 21st century. As Sr. Regina Haney, OSF, Executive Director of the National Association of Boards of Catholic Education has stated, "First you must see to it that the right people are sitting around the table."

Local policy will usually determine whether governing boards are elected or appointed by the principal and/or pastor. In arguing for appointed boards to deal with Church issues, William O'Malley, S.J. recently wrote in *America*:

> ...these should be people who are the most capable (at the tasks to be undertaken)—people who are invited, not elected, since popularity is not the primary component of their service but rather commitment, wits and imagination. (p.10)

If, however, board members must be elected, it behooves the principal to insist that all potential candidates be in-serviced in what their role in governance will be and the high expectations that the community holds for those entrusted with such an awesome responsibility. Only after being fully advised of their roles and responsibilities should candidates' names be placed on the ballot.

The National Congress on Catholic Schools for the Twenty-first century determined that one of the primary roles of school boards is "supervising and monitoring the philosophy and mission of the school." (NCEA, 1991) The principal must provide leadership so that the board assumes this rightful role. The key to success is for the board to feel both ownership of and responsibility for the mission.

The principal can take specific steps to encourage ownership and responsibility.

Reinvolvement in issues of substance

Deep ownership comes through the learning that arises from engagement in solving problems. (Fullan, 1993) The board's sense of ownership will increase as it takes part in decision-making on issues of importance. Nothing motivates a board more than seeing that results have been achieved through actions they have taken and suggestions they have made. Seeing that they do, indeed, make a difference and have had a measurable impact on strengthening the school gives board members a sense of ownership and a feeling of pride in the school community.

Active participation in matters of importance helps the board formulate the vision of the school as well. "People need a good deal of reflective experience before they can form a plausible vision. Vision emerges from, more than it precedes, action." (Fullan, 1993, p. 127)

Building of consensus

Groups will not reach quality decisions by taking shortcuts. The principal must guide the board as it takes the longer route through consensus. The principal must assume leadership in seeing that those who sit around the table have an openness to participation, an openness to diversity, an openness to conflict, an openness to reflection, and even an openness to mistakes. (Patterson, 1993) Group decisions reached through consensus enhance a sense of ownership. Principals, however, should not lose sight of the fact that the process of merging personal and shared visions takes time. (Fullan, 1993)

Development of trust

Because cohesive boards work most effectively, principals must work at developing a sense of trust among board members. Often this can be done through modeling. When board members realize that the principal values the suggestions and opinions they offer and respects the decisions they have made, they are most willing to make a serious commitment of their time and talents to the various board committees. The trust engendered will become mutual, and the principal will consistently find the board to be among the school's most enthusiastic advocates.

An honest sharing of information, in the difficult times as well as in moments of celebration, promotes the development of trust as well. The principal will find a true sense of strength in board members who realize that they have been trusted to share events of significance.

Opportunities for responsibility

The board can't develop a sense of responsibility for the mission of the school if it has not taken responsibility for projects and actions which flow from the mission statement. The principal must assume leadership in giving the board such opportunities. In addition to working on the budget and policy statements, the board should be actively involved in special projects which they or the principal identify as having a significant impact on the school. Boards could easily take responsibility for conceptualizing effective endowment campaigns, developing five-year enrollment plans, identifying community needs with which classes might choose to become involved, or developing a plan for impacting policy. Involvement in special projects in accord with the school's stated mission increases the board's sense of responsibility for the mission.

A bold new future

As we continue to strengthen the role of the laity, as we take specific steps to share the governance of schools with them, we should begin to prepare for the possibility of entirely new governance forms.

Perhaps the 21st century will see the advent of schools governed entirely by lay boards: school systems in which bishops, pastors, and principals voluntarily limit themselves to spiritual and educational leadership while school boards take on ownership and responsibility for all other aspects.

The young people who attend Catholic schools are their children, their grandchildren, their nieces and nephews, their sisters and brothers and cousins. It is a matter of simple justice that the schools be their schools in some real, instead of symbolic, sense. (Greeley, 1992, p. 238)

It will not be an easy road, but we must begin the journey if we are to be faithful to the documents of the Council, the declarations of the National Council, and the gospel of the Lord Jesus Christ.

Resources

Bonstingl, John Jay, *Schools of Quality: An Introduction to Total Quality Management in Education*, Alexandria, VA, Association for Supervision and Curriculum Development, 1992.

Buetow, Harold A., *A History of United States Catholic Schooling*, Washington, DC, National Catholic Educational Association, 1985.

Fullan, Michael, "Innovation, Reform, and Restructuring Strategies," *Challenges and Achievements of American Education, The 1993 ASCD Yearbook*, Alexandria, VA, Association for Supervision and Curriculum Development, 1993.

Greeley, Andrew M., "A Modest Proposal for the Reform of Catholic Schools," *America*, Vol. 166 No. 10, March 21-28, 1992.

Indrisano, Roselmina, "The Excellence Ethos and the Leadership Role," In R. J. Kealey (Ed.), *Reflections on the Role of the Catholic School Principal*, Washington, DC, National Catholic Eductional Association, 1989.

O'Malley, William J., "The Church of the Faithful," America, Vol. 168 No. 21, June 19-26, 1993.

"National Congress: Catholic Schools for the 21st Century" *School Governance and Finance*, Washington, DC, National Catholic Educational Association, 1991.

Patterson, Jerry L., *Leadership for Tomorrow's Schools*, Alexandria, VA, Association for Supervision and Curriculum Development, 1993.

Sheehan, Lourdes, *Building Better Boards*, Washington, DC, National Catholic Educational Association, 1990.

Smith, Wilma F. and Andrews, Richard, *Instructional Leadership: How Principals Make a Difference*, Alexandria, VA, Association for Supervison and Curriculum Development, 1989.

Margaret E. Curran
All Souls Catholic School
Sanford, Florida

Section IV
Catholic Identity

Nurturing the
Faith Life of Students
through a
Developmental
Religion Plan

We call Christ the Master Teacher. What made Him such a Master Teacher? What "methods" did He use that we, too, must adopt if we are to touch the minds and hearts of our children today?

During His brief three years as the Master Teacher, Christ gathered His students closely around Him and instructed them in simple, human style. He began by building a foundation based on their previous experiences. His students were rooted in Jewish law and tradition. Christ gently moved them from this experience to a new one, into the new law, the new covenant, which was a higher level of maturity in their faith journey.

What is our plan as teachers following in the steps of the Master Teacher? In the words of the document *To Teach As Jesus Did,* Christian education is intended to "make one's faith become living, conscious, and active through the light of instruction." Our plan must have as its overall goal to help our students on their faith journey, moving them gently as the Master Teacher did to bring them to a higher level of maturity. How do we do that with our students today?

We know that Catholic religious education must reflect the teaching of the Church as articulated in Church documents. *To Teach As Jesus Did* states:

> "The educational mission of the Church is an integrated ministry embracing three interlocking dimensions: the message revealed by God which the Church proclaims; fellowship in the life of the Holy Spirit; service to the Christian community and the entire human community."

The Appleton Catholic Educational System of Appleton, Wisconsin designed a plan to meet the needs of our students on their faith journey.

Steps in designing this plan

STEP ONE: A religion curriculum committee was formed. Committee membership consisted of
- one principal, chairperson
- two teachers from each of the five campuses in the system
- two Religion Education Directors
- one Religion teacher from the local Catholic high school
- one Diocesan Religion Consultant

STEP TWO: Tasks of the committee were chosen. These tasks were to
- Formulate a system-wide mission statement for our Religion curriculum based on our system's philosophy and diocesan philosophy
- Formulate the system's religion curriculum guide based on the diocesan religion curriculum
- Select resources, including a text where apppropriate
- Design an implementation plan, including a staff development plan

STEP THREE: Set a time frame for meetings and completion of tasks.

STEP FOUR: Formulation of our mission statement. Our school system based its mission statement on this three-fold purpose.

The Appleton Catholic Educational System finds its reason and purpose for existence within the context of the mission of the Church based on the document *To Teach As Jesus Did*. Our purpose has a three-fold mission which is
- first, to impart the message of Jesus Christ
- second, to advance the building of Christian community
- third, to implement the message of Jesus through service to others.

Mission statement for religion curriculum
Appleton Catholic Educational System
The Appleton Catholic Educational System believes that the entire Christian community including parents, students, teachers, and

staff are called to respond to Christ's invitation to follow Him. Together we hold a shared responsibility to live out the dictate of Christ which is to go and teach all nations. (Matt.28:19-20) As a Catholic Christian community, we teach the gospel message of Jesus, build community, and live the faith through service to the parish, local, and world community. Through worship, scripture, and tradition, our Religion curriculum builds upon each stage of human and faith development. We challenge our students to grow in their Catholic faith and to go forth to create a world in harmony with the Gospel message.

STEP FIVE: Formulate the belief statements for each age level.

Once the mission statement was formulated, the committee proceeded to write belief statements for each grade level based on the three-fold mission of the Church: Message, Community, and Service.

These belief statements were developed not only by committee members but also by grade level teachers at each campus. Each committee member was commissioned to meet with grade level teachers in each school. Returning to the committee, the belief statements were critiqued for each age level, assuring continuity and developmental readiness.

Belief statements according to age and grade level: Preschool—three years old

Message:
a. We believe that God loves us and is always with us.
b. We believe that God loves us and is with us when we pray and have fun.
c. We believe that God loves us and is with us when we're at home and when we're away from home.
d. We believe that God loves us and is with us as we grow and learn new things.

Community:
a. We believe that God is with us through other people.
b. We believe that God is with us in our families.
c. We believe that God is with us when we interact with our classmates.

Service:
a. We believe that God is with us when we help our families, classmates, and other people.
b. We believe that God is with us when we care for our pets.

Preschool—four years old

Message:
a. We believe that God helps us appreciate ourselves.
b. We believe that God helps us enjoy living.
c. We believe that God helps us learn new things.
d. We believe that God helps us be friends with others.

Community:
a. We believe that God helps us be friends to children.
b. We believe that God helps us be friends to grown-ups.
c. We believe that God helps us be friends to neighbors.
d. We believe that God helps us be friends to animals.

Service:
a. We believe that God helps us care for ourselves.
b. We believe that God helps us care for our families.
c. We believe that God helps us care for our pets.
d. We believe that God helps us care for our things.

Kindergarten

Message:
a. We believe that God created the universe.
b. We believe that God makes us unique and that our bodies, our feelings, our talents, and our senses are gifts from God.
c. We believe that God created people who love us and help us.
d. We believe that through biblical stories we learn about God's greatest gift, Jesus, who loves us and teaches us.

Community:
a. We believe that God has given us many people to love - families, friends, teachers, neighbors, community helpers.
b. We believe that these people show love and concern for us just as God does.
c. We believe that God's love is a reason to celebrate together as family and friends.
d. We believe that we gather at Mass to celebrate, to give thanks, and to listen to the stories of Jesus.

Service:
a. We believe that we are called to take care of the gifts of God's creation.
b. We believe that we praise God when we share our talents and use our senses.
c. We believe that Jesus shows us how to love and help others.
d. We believe that God's love teaches us to love God, ourselves, and others.

Grade one

Message:
a. We believe that the Bible is a special way to know God as a loving Father who created all things.
b. We believe that Jesus is God's own Son who came to earth to show us God's love.
c. We believe that through Baptism we are members of the Catholic Church and belong to God's family in this Church.
d. We believe that celebrations and the receiving of God's special gifts through the Spirit are a part of the Church.

Community:
a. We believe that we are to appreciate God's creation and take care of it.
b. We believe that we are to live as Jesus did by treating others with respect and kindness.
c. We believe that we are to be responsible members of God's family, our own families, our school and parish family.
d. We believe that we need to learn about our parish and what we can do to be active members.

Service:
a. We believe that we are good stewards when we help make the world a better place by showing care for God's creation.
b. We believe that we follow the example of Jesus by being kind and loving toward each other.
c. We believe that we are to contribute to family life and develop an attitude of self-giving.
d. We believe that we spread the light of God's love by caring for others and doing good to all people.

Grade two

Message:
a. We believe that God creates everything good, sent His Son, Jesus, our model whom we follow and who gives the Holy Spirit, who guides us in our lives.
b. We believe that God is a forgiving God and we are called to forgive one another.
c. We believe that Eucharist is the Mass, during which we listen to God's word, respond to it, and give thanks.
d. We believe that Jesus is with us in Holy Communion and gives Himself in the sharing of the bread and wine as He did at the Last Supper.

Community
a. We believe that a community is a group of people who work and pray together.
b. We believe that Baptism is the sacrament of welcome into our Catholic Christian community.
c. We believe that forgiveness or reconciliation helps us to be peacemakers in our communities.
d. We believe that we come together at Mass to pray as a Catholic Christian community.

Service:
a. We believe that God's word at Mass teaches us to share with others.
b. We believe that God's word at Mass teaches us to respect and care for all creation.
c. We believe that the Mass calls us forth to make a better world.
d. We believe that the Mass sends us forth to love and help others.

Grade three

Message:
a. We believe that God has a special love for each of us and has sent the Son, Jesus, as our Savior.
b. We believe that Jesus sent the Holy Spirit and gave us the sacraments to help us live as God's people.
c. We believe that the writings of the books of the Bible were inspired by God, and that the life and teachings of Jesus have been recorded in the New Testament.
d. We believe that prayer is talking and listening to God for the purpose of giving praise, giving thanks, asking for help, and seeking forgiveness.

Community:
a. We believe that we are welcomed into God's family at Baptism and are promised help to grow in our Catholic faith.
b. We believe that the sacraments are powerful signs through which Jesus shares God's life with us.
c. We believe that the people of God, the Church, began in Jesus' time and grows as we spread the good news of Jesus.
d. We believe that celebrating the Mass as a community is the greatest prayer of praise and thanksgiving.

Grade four

Message:
a. We believe that we are to live as Catholic Christians.
b. We believe that the commandments and beatitudes of justice and peace are God's laws and guides to living.
c. We believe that we are invited to be disciples of Jesus and bring fullness of life to others.
d. We believe that God's merciful love and forgiveness are revealed in Scripture and tradition.

Community:
a. We believe that the world we live in is beautiful and we must work in community to save and protect it.
b. We believe that as a community we are called to worship God, care for others as the Good Samaritan did and show our love for God when we help those in need.
c. We believe that by telling the truth, respecting ourselves, others and all living things, we show reverence for God's presence within community.
d. We believe that, as a community, we become more closely united when we celebrate Eucharist.

Service:
a. We believe that when we practice the beatitudes we are living as our best selves, emphasizing our interactions with others at home and school.
b. We believe that we show our love for God in honoring, respecting, and serving God.
c. We believe that when we live our faith, we love and respect ourselves and others, care for material possessions, and we tell the truth.
d. We believe that as a Church we commit ourselves to involvement and service in the local and world community in such ministries as Adopt-A-Family, rice meal, and mission collections.

Grade five

Message:
a. We believe that Jesus is the sacrament of God's presence and asks the Church to carry on His mission.
b. We believe that we are invited by the Church to receive the Sacraments of Initiation—Baptism, Eucharist, and Confirmation.
c. We believe that we are called to and celebrate in community the sacraments of healing and service—Reconciliation, Anointing of the Sick, Matrimony, and Holy Orders.
d. We believe that the Scriptures call us to become a community of faith, hope, and love.

Community:
a. We believe that through Baptism we are welcomed into a community of believers.
b. We believe that by celebrating the Eucharist we are able to nurture others and reunite divisions in the community.
c. We believe that we experience the healing of ourselves and the community through the Sacraments of Reconciliation and the Anointing of the Sick.
d. We believe that the sacraments of Confirmation, Matrimony and Holy Orders will enable us to grow in our faith as adult members of the community.

Service:
a. We believe that the sacraments are the basis for our service in community.
b. We believe that we carry on Jesus' work by doing service for others in our school and community.
c. We believe that we carry on Christ's ministry by living as Jesus did.
d. We believe that we grow in our faith through study, participation, and service.

Grade six

Message:
a. We believe that Christianity shares the same scriptural foundation as Judaism.
b. We believe that the Bible is worthy of reverence.
c. We believe that the role of the prophets is significant in salvation history and we are called to be prophets.
d. We believe that Jesus is prophet, priest, and king.

Community:
a. We believe that the prophets and Jesus administered to others and we are called to minister to the world.
b. We believe that following Scriptural models we relate to one another with trust and respect.
c. We believe that each person in the community needs to experience private and communal prayer.
d. We believe that active participation in liturgies and prayer services is a preparation for future involvement as adults in the Catholic Church.

Service:
a. We believe that all must be given an opportunity to serve throughout the community.
b. We believe that awareness of the greater world, its needs, and our role in it leads us to action.
c. We believe that it is our responsibility to use our talents to carry out the Scriptural message.
d. We believe that our service to others needs to be respectful and compassionate.

Grade seven

Message:
a. We believe that the study of Judaism enhances our understanding of our Catholic Christian faith.
b. We believe that through the study of the four gospels we grow in our understanding of the life, times, and teachings of Jesus.
c. We believe that Jesus invites us to discipleship.
d. We believe that the reflective study of Scripture and Catholic doctrine encourages our growth in faith and moral decision-making.

Community:
a. We believe that sharing our faith experiences within the school community helps us develop a positive self-image.
b. We believe that we need to develop a sensitivity to the needs of others.
c. We believe that we are called to accept, respect, and use talents for the good of our school, parish, and community.
d. We believe that we grow in our understanding of Church and community through involvement in our home parish.

Service:
a. We believe that we form a Christian bond of friendship with the broader community through outreach activities.
b. We believe that by sharing our personal possessions we are living the message of Christ.
c. We believe that through the sharing of our time and talents we develop a sense of Christian stewardship.
d. We believe that we are called to minister to others both spiritually and materially.

Grade eight

Message:
a. We believe that a key image today is people of God.
b. We believe that knowledge of our roots and tradition enriches our personal faith development.
c. We believe that studying Church history enables us to better understand today's church.
d. We believe that the people and events found in Scripture and Church history influence what we believe and practice as Catholics today.

Community:
a. We believe that the lives of real people past and present make known the message of Jesus within the Church community.
b. We believe that we must develop a sensitivity to the needs of the larger world.
c. We believe that we need to realize the consequences of sins of ommision, especially in community.
d. We believe that each of us has an impact on our school, parish, and community.

Service:
a. We believe that service is an outgrowth of faith and personal convictions.
b. We believe that the desire to do service must become an integral part of our Christian life.
c. We believe that justice calls us to provide for the common good.
d. We believe that the call to charity and justice enables one to "walk in someone else's shoes."

STEP SIX: Areas of curriculum development

On completion of the Basic Statements, it was our concern that in the Appleton Catholic Educational System we convey the authentic message of the Church through the teaching of doctrine, celebration of the liturgical year, study of scripture, and development of prayer. The Master Plan included four areas of development: doctrines of our faith, liturgical year, forms of prayer, and biblical.

Doctrines of Faith	**Liturgical Year**
Ten Commandments	Advent
Sacraments	Christmas/Epiphany
Beatitudes	Lent
Nicene Creed	Easter
	Pentecost
	Ordinary Time

Forms of Prayer	**Biblical**
Praise	Bible Stories
Thanksgiving	Scripture
Sorrow	Biblical Prayer
Petition	Study of Scripture

STEP SEVEN: Development of prayer

We desired to have all of our students be knowledgeable of our traditional Catholic prayers. We listed these, distinguishing between public and private prayer and between those that were to be an integral part of our religion curriculum and those that could be integrated at the discretion of each campus.

STEP EIGHT: Scope and sequence for prayer development

In the Appleton Catholic Educational System, prayer, in its varied forms, is taught as central to spiritual development. The code we used was adopted from our Green Bay Diocesan Religion Guide. Each grade level reflected the growth in maturity of the students.

CODE: R - Readiness experiences

I - Introduce—Present initial concepts and/or skills

P - Develop concepts, wording, and practice of skills

M - Correct knowledge of wording and/or gesture

W - Wording

U - Used consistently

STEP NINE: Choice of texts

Each campus was free to adopt a textbook that they believed was in keeping with our Master Plan of spiritual development for our students.

STEP TEN: Staff development

A formal presentation of the religion curriculum guide was given at the beginning of the school year. Each staff member received a copy. Committee members from each campus were responsible for in-servicing staff members. Since staff members had been actively involved in the plan, ownership for the plan was already there.

Staff development continues through on-going in-services. Staff members are required to gain religion certification. This can be done through college credits, CEU'S, or clock hours. Any course work for religion certification must include theology, Scripture, and psychology/methodology.

While we, as teachers in the Appleton Catholic Educational System, grow in our ability to teach as our model and Master Teacher, Jesus, we must also realize the we are His "students." We must listen and learn from Him as He gently gathers us to Himself, moving us to higher levels of maturity in our own faith journey. Only then can we be effective teachers of religion touching both the minds and hearts of our students.

Resources

To Teach As Jesus Did
Pastoral Message on Catholic Education
National Conference of Catholic Bishops, November, 1972

Sharing the Light of Faith
National Catechetical Directory for Catholics in the United States
November, 1977

Green Bay Diocesan Religion Curriculum Guidelines, 1989

Religion Curriculum Guide, 1991
Appleton Catholic Educational System

Sister Mary Barbara Loch
St. Thomas More School
Appleton, Wisconsin

Value the Difference

It is a growing perception of many across our country today that there is a difference in our Catholic schools. What is that difference? Is it an excellence in academics? Is it an atmosphere where discipline and orderliness are expected? Is it the opportunity to pass on the teachings of the Catholic Church? Is it the high involvement and support of parents and parishioners? Is it the dedication of teachers who usually work for pay much less than their public school counterparts? Yes, yes, yes, yes, and yes! All of these factors are part of what makes the Catholic school different.

There is a foundation, however, upon which all of these are built. The Congregation for Catholic Education writes from Rome in 1988 that, "while the Catholic school is like any other school...there is one essential difference: it draws its inspiration and its strength from the Gospel in which it is rooted."

The inspiration and strength of the gospel must be nurtured. It is the spiritual formation of the entire school which is the essential dimension of the Catholic school. (National Congress on Catholic Schools for the 21st century) Administrators and teachers in Catholic schools must value the importance of nurturing the spiritual life of each of our students—from the youngest to the oldest.

We owe it to children to give them the experience of building a relationship with an all-holy, all-loving, invisible, but always-present God. Children need to discover God in their own lives. They need leaders who will guide them into a closer relationship and more intimate conversation with God in prayer.

Sometimes our teachers, especially those new to our schools do not feel adequate with leading prayer for their students. Yet we read in *Sharing the Light of Faith* that by the very nature of their ministry catechists (teachers) are often called to lead the community in prayer. Even though the teacher is a pray-er, it is sometimes difficult to cross over into a child's spirituality.

What can a principal do to help teachers recognize their roles as prayer-leaders and feel comfortable in that role?

Modeling prayer leadership. Just as a teacher is leader of prayer in the classroom, the principal is leader of prayer for the faculty and staff. It is important to assume that role at faculty meetings, scheduled staff prayer gatherings, and times of special need, thanksgiving or joy. Using a variety of prayer forms lets teachers know there are many ways to pray. Some will fit an individual's style more than others.

Providing Resources. Many books and periodicals discussing children's prayer are available. It is helpful to have a variety of these available for teachers' use. While teachers may not want to use a particular prayer "as is," it may be a springboard for ideas. Often detailed suggestions are given on how to prepare children for prayer, or what materials to use.

Offering Opportunities to Lead Prayer. As educators, we know we learn by doing. It is valuable to ask teachers to lead prayer for the faculty or students as they feel comfortable. To hear the principals' affirmation of a "job well done" can give a teacher the confidence needed to continue as prayer leader.

Inviting Teachers to Grow in their Own Spirituality. Gentle invitations from a principal to deepen one's own spirituality may be the encouragement a teacher needs. As principals, we can nurture our teachers by a short reflection in our weekly bulletin, our prayer to-gether as faculty, a scheduled annual teachers' retreat, our informal conversations, and our reverence for the spirituality already present in each teacher.

Whole school prayer

There are many opportunities to gather together the whole school for prayer. Often schools will begin or end the day with prayer over the P.A. In small schools sometimes students are brought together physically to open the day with prayer or to be sent home with God's blessings. Sometimes an adult may lead the prayer. At other times students have been prepared to be prayer leaders.

Church feastdays or civic celebrations may be the occasion for all-school prayer. At the beginning of the year students and classrooms may be blessed. The feast of St. Francis gives an opportunity for a blessing of pets. Children love to celebrate birthdays—a perfect chance for monthly birthday blessings. Some examples of other occasions are Thanksgiving prayer, blessing and planting a tree for Arbor Day, lighting Advent wreaths, special prayer celebrations for Catholic Schools Week, Stations of the Cross for Lent, Epiphany blessing of classrooms, Marian prayer service for Mary, living rosary for October, perhaps sending off a parishioner to visit a sister parish in a Third

World country. Almost any special event can be a time to give praise to God and to ask for blessing.

Of course, the size of the school may limit the total school gatherings. However, schools may want to gather in grade levels, to pair younger and older grades, to include first-floor or second-floor gatherings—whatever might give a sense of the larger body at prayer.

Classroom prayer

One author characterizes the ministry of catechesis as being like a relationship of a trade master and an apprentice—with the teacher being the "master" Christian and the student the "apprentice" Christian. The apprentice not only needs to know about prayer but must also master the skills and the art of praying. A classroom teacher provides a child the opportunities to practice prayer skills with more and more regularity.

It is helpful for a teacher to set goals for classroom prayer at the beginning of a school year. How will the teacher make a place for prayer in the classroom—perhaps a prayer table, or prayer corner? When will prayer take place? Most teachers have a set routine for certain prayers. In addition how does the teacher include other prayer forms and give the motivation for them?

Some prayer forms which can be used with children are: guided imagery, shared prayer, scriptural prayer, musical prayer, journaling, gesturing prayer, choral speaking, letters to God, audio-visual prayer, prayer scrapbook, intercessory prayer, or silent relaxation in the hand of God.

These are only examples of prayer. Anything which brings teachers and children in touch with God's presence can be prayer. Being aware of God's touch in every person, thing, or event in life is the beginning of prayer. Our response to that awareness completes the prayer.

Liturgical prayer is certainly a vital part of the spiritual formation of children. However, the limits of this article do not permit a further exploration at this time. Extensive materials on the subject are available and can be very helpful to a classroom teacher.

With regard to prayer, it is important to know the capacities and limits of the age groups we teach. We remember that classic principle that grace builds on nature. Growth in a child's spiritual life depends on the child's mental, psychological, and emotional growth.

Characteristics of the prayer of younger children (Grades K-4)
Faith is naive and innocent. Encourage the wonder and belief.
  • A beautiful simplicity is the hallmark of a child's faith. Prayer, too, must be uncomplicated.

- A young child's attention span or vocabulary must be taken into consideration when preparing prayer.
- Don't expect "too much too soon." Start out with small steps.
- Draw the child into prayer with song, movement, activities— as well as words and silence.

Characteristics of prayer with older children (Grades 5-8)

Middle school students are "in-between kids," and have a strong need for a solid spiritual life.

- Because middle-school students are caught up in a busy, fast-paced, over-stimulated society, they need a sense of personal solitude.
- Prayer must give young people opportunities to explore themselves.
- Prayer must be taught—by being introduced to many forms through actual practice.
- Prayer must help our youth face the negatives of life and use them as opportunities for growth.

Our children in Catholic schools need prayer—they need a spiritual life. If Catholic schools help them to discover and build up their relationship with God, their young lives will be changed. They will become rooted in the Gospel values which inspire and strengthen them. They will truly value the difference.

Resources

Brokamp, Marilyn, O.S.F., *Prayer Times For Primary Grades*, St. Anthony Messenger Press, Cincinnati, OH, 1987.

Hesch, John B., *Prayer and Meditation for Middle School Kids*, Paulist Press, Mahwah, NY, 1985.

Jessie, Karen, *Praying With Children Grades 1-3*, The Center for Learning, Villa Maria, PA, 1986.

Jessie, Karen, *Praying With Children Grades 4-6*, The Center for Learning, Villa Maria, PA, 1986.

The National Congress on Catholic Schools for the Twenty-first Century, National Catholic Educational Association, Washington, DC, 1991.

Reehorst, Jane, B.V.M., *Guided Meditations for Children*, Wm. C. Brown Communications, Inc., Dubuque, IA, 1986.

The Religious Dimension of Education in a Catholic School, The Congregation for Catholic Education, Rome, 1988.

Reichert, Richard, *Teaching Tips for Religion Teachers Grades 1-3, Grades 4-8,* Our Sunday Visitor, Inc., Huntington, IN, 1989.

Sister Pat Gavin
St. Monica School
Mishawaka, Indiana

Community —
A Garden of Faith

We often receive plant kits as gifts, such as, an herb garden that contains all the components needed to bring about a finished product — seeds, soil, containers, and directions. But nothing is accomplished until we pick it up and put time and effort into putting it all together.

God's gift of a school faith community is a little like the kit. He gives us the people to work with and the faith of these people. It is up to us, with our students and faculty, to bring together our faith, time, and effort to create a faith community that is ever changing, ever new.

Community building is a shared task that all members of the community must take responsibility for. Some guidelines for nurturing would include

- Sharing the vision of principal and faculty
- Cultivating the strengths of each person
- Making a commitment with a positive attitude
- Realizing we are not perfect
- Taking risks
- Understanding that time is needed to develop a strong faith community.

Evelyn Eaton Whitehead and James D. Whitehead state in *Community of Faith*, "As followers of Jesus we hunger for community, for a home where our faith finds nourishment. We yearn for a gathering that welcomes our gifts and respects our wounds. We long for an assembly that can enkindle our faith in the face of an often cold world."

Keeping this in mind, the principal and the faculty should share their vision of the importance of community. One way of doing this that we have found very useful is the NCEA program, *Sharing the Faith: A Faculty Progam for Catholic Schools.*

This comprehensive faculty faith development program consisting of 12 reflective sessions was developed to be implemented over two years, six sessions for each year. The six sessions, used throughout the year, begin with a retreat day. The last session comes at the end of the year, and at this time, the faculty consider, "Shall we do this again next year?" Many faculties find the program nurturing and supportive of their faith, an initial step to shaping a collaborative vision of the school.

As with the soil for the herb garden, we need to cultivate the strengths of each of the faculty members to carry out the vision we have created. Brainstorming with the faculty as to how this vision can be carried out, not only among themselves but also with the students, brings out the strengths of each of the faculty members as they build on each others' ideas of one another.

Noted here are some of the ideas that have come from such brainstorming.

- Development of a school theme around some value such as "God Loves a Cheerful Giver" for encouraging service among students.
- Encouragement of students to put forth their best effort in all aspects of school life: honors assemblies, Terrific Kids Awards, leadership club, and a buddy system.
- Recognition of the teachers' needs for professional growth through attendance at workshops, visiting classrooms in other schools, and monetary allowances for college courses.

The herb garden requires certain conditions for growth, and so too, a faith community requires certain elements in order to flourish in a school. The principal and faculty need to have a positive attitude, be willing to take risks in opening up to one another, and understanding that all of this takes time to develop and grow.

Faculty involvement in developing faith community has a dynamic rippling effect within the entire school. It builds self-esteem, and morale which flows over to the students. In the end, principal, faculty, and students become a living sign of Catholic identity — a flourishing garden of faith.

Resources

Johnson, Evelyn M. R. & Bobbie Bower, *Building a Great Children's Ministry*, Abingdon Press, Nashville, TN, 1992.

Sharing the Faith: A Faculty Program for Catholic Schools, NCEA, Washington, DC, 1992.

Taylor, Audrey and Joe, *Families Exploring Faith: A Parents' Guide to the Older Adolescent Years,* Don Bosco Multimedia, New Rochelle, NY, 1992.

Whitehead, Evelyn Eaton and James D., *Community of Faith,* Twenty-Third Publications, Mystic, CT, 1992.

Sister Mary Ann Hart
St. Sylvester Central School
Woodsfield, Ohio

Sister M. Frederica Polanski
St. John De LaSalle School
Niagara Falls, New York

Service Projects:
A Smorgasbord of
Opportunity

Violence has become a part of our daily lives. We see it on the news, in movies, on television, and more recently, we are seeing more acts of violence erupting in the school setting. The Rodney King incident in Los Angeles graphically illustrated racial violence in the news. Ninja Turtles and the more recent Jurassic Park movie are causing some to question the amount of violence viewed by children today. Cartoons introduce violence prior to the age of two in most households. The movie "Lean on Me," in which the principal wields a baseball bat, shocked many Americans into the reality that drugs and violence were becoming commonplace, especially in the inner cities.

This prevalence of violence in society is all the more reason we should be communicating the message of peace and the idea of living in harmony with one another to children in our schools. *To Teach as Jesus Did* identifies three characteristics of quality Catholic education: message, community, and service. As Robert Kealey states in his book *Apostolic Service Activities for Catholic Elementary School Students,* "an effective Catholic education program proclaims to the student the message of the Gospel. Students so internalize this message that they live in harmony with each other, they have community with one another." This shared life impels the students to serve one another.

If it is the goal of Catholic schools to have students live in harmony, it is worth our time to explore ways in which students can be taught to value each other and humanity.

If parents, teachers, and administrators believe service to be an effective way in which students can internalize the concepts of peace and brotherhood, then the school should seriously consider effective ways in which meaningful service projects can be successfully integrated into the educational program.

Service is a complex biblical idea that is essential to our life as Christians. As part of our educational process we need to prepare the whole child to take on this Christian role in society. Service-learning provides a way of unifying concepts with real life experiences.

Selling the idea

Most parochial schools, and more recently many public schools, (see *Education Week,* March 3, 1993) see the value of service projects. Educators realize that students acquire knowledge, skills, and responsibility through hands-on learning which stems from service projects. When students are involved in decision-making and develop caring attitudes through personal involvement, it is not uncommon to see the students' self-esteem rise. Children with high levels of self-esteem are more likely to become peacemakers in society.

Educating parents about the value of service projects within the school setting is the first step a school should take when planning the integration process. This information should be shared through letters or at a Home and School Organization meeting. In addition to the skills discussed earlier, community service projects teach valuable lessons about the responsibilities of citizenship which help to create a sense of concern for public good, so essential to the future of the United States. Social Studies skills, including data gathering, critical thinking, group interaction and leadership are just some of the positive outcomes which can be pointed out to parents.

It shouldn't be difficult convincing teachers of service integration benefits. Studies have shown that students involved in learning experiences outside the classroom have a higher success rate in school and are encouraged to develop higher order thinking skills. More important to teachers would be the nuts and bolts of how to integrate service projects into the daily curriculum.

Integrating the service project into the curriculum

The following steps should be taken when considering service projects with classes or groups.

- Identify the goal of the class or group. Ask "Why do the project?"
- Identify the need. Is it of value to the community? (Research local service opportunities available within the school and community.)
- Involve the students in the decision-making details.
- Determine how the project could be integrated into subject area(s).
- Determine the number of students needed for the project.
- Clear the project with the appropriate school and community officials.
- Evaluate the service project.

The following are examples of successful service projects used in various schools and how they were intertwined in classroom teaching.

Math

To generate funds for the Ronald McDonald House, soda tabs were collected and money donated per pound. The students counted and sorted the tabs into tens, hundreds, and thousands. The tabs were put in various sized containers and estimating was done. The students also measured out lengths of tabs laid into feet, yards, centimeters, etc. For story word problems, the students used tabs for subtraction, addition and so forth. (Patti Fischer, 2nd grade, St. Joseph School, Jefferson City, MO)

Science/religion

The effects of drug abuse and how it takes its toll on the body's organs, the psychological dependency, and the physical addiction were studied in the primary department of the school. K-2 students cut pictures from magazines and pasted them on grocery sacks from a local store. The pictures illustrated change in expressions (from happy to sad), or in family lifestyle. This project could also fit into religion class in teaching 'right' from 'wrong.' (Teresa Holland, 1st grade, St. Joseph School, Jefferson City, MO)

Language arts

In response to a request by the Russian Education Department to help develop the skills Russian children needed in a free economy, the school counselor developed joint educational projects. Second grade students sent four page notes and cards to Russian children of the same age. The cards included both letters and drawings about themselves: "This is me," "These are things I like," "These are things that upset me," and "These are my friends." These items were exchanged with the children in Russia. Pictures were taken of the two groups and then exchanged. The primary goal of the project was to help children see the commonality of their likes and dislikes and to appreciate the fact that both groups have frustrations and negative experiences. A child derives psychological strength to cope with stress if he/she sees a problem as a difficulty of 'children' and not as the result of an unknown peculiarity about themselves. By integrating activities to improve coping skills and self esteem into the existing curriculum, the labeling problem which school officials face is avoided. (Mary Lou O'Brien, School Counselor, St. Joseph School, Jefferson City, MO)

Social studies

Upper grade students became "guardian angels" to senior daily Mass-goers by sitting with them once a week at morning Mass, thus cementing relationships between students and seniors in the parish. This relationship developed over a year with both parties learning more about each other. In another setting, 8th grade students provided breakfast on first Fridays of each month after Mass. This service not only broke down barriers between the parish and school, but allowed the students to see that relationships can be built through subtle actions. (Charlotte Smith, 8th Grade Teacher, Our Lady of Mount Carmel, Niagara Falls, NY)

Home economics

In Our Lady of the Snows School, junior high students baked bread from scratch, measuring ingredients, doubling recipes, calculating ingredients, and working together cooperatively to provide school guests with a brunch. This project was duplicated in a larger school setting with the students working together with their business partners in the city.

On the national level, the Civic Achievement Award Program (CAAP) provides examples of community service projects for fifth through eighth grade students. (For more information see the article "The Civic Achievement Award Program: Civic Learning for Adolescents through Research Writing and Community Service.")

One can easily see how projects can be integrated into any subject. Most projects fit nicely into the religion curriculum, but with a little creativity can be expanded into other areas of teaching.

Evaluating the project

Assessing a service project after the completion is the final step. Teachers, as well as students should answer the following questions:
- Was the goal met?
- How were we able to help others?
- What was learned from the service project?
- How do I feel about the outcome?

Conclusion

Service projects without meaning can be mere busy work. Meaningful service projects integrated into the curriculum with goals and a purpose can be a way for children to internalize the concepts of peace and living in harmony with one another as adults. We must never lose sight of the example of Christ the servant or the attitude we should have in our hearts as we serve.

"I have set an example that you should do as I have done to You." (Jn 13:15)

Resources

Dickie, Steve and Pearson, Darrell, *Creative Programming Ideas for Junior High Ministry*, Youth Specialties, Inc. 1992.

Glenn, H. Stephen and Nelsen, Jane, *Raising Self-Reliant Children in a Self-Indulgent World*, Prima Publishing and Communications, 1989.

Goldman, Eric and Langan, Terri, "Civic Perspective," Fall 1990, *The Civic Achievement Award Program: Civic Learning for Adolescents through Research, Writing, and Community Service*, 1990.

Guerin, Marisa, *The Junior High Connection*, Washington, DC, The National CYO Federation, 1978.

Kealey, Robert J., *Apostolic Service Activities for Catholic Elementary School Students*, Washington, DC, NCEA, 1988.

Kirby, Kathleen, *ERIC Digest*, "Community Service and Civic Education," Bloomington, IN, *ERIC Clearinghouse for Social Studies Education*, 1989.

Larsen, Sandy, *Any Old Time Book 9*, Victor Books.

Lawton, Millicent, *Education Week*, "Providence to Open High School Devoted to Community Service," March 3, 1993.

McPherson, Kate and Mary Nebgen, *Education and Urban Society*, May 1991, "Connections: Community Service and School Reform Recommendations," 1991.

National Conference of Catholic Bishops, *To Teach as Jesus Did*, United States Catholic Conference, Washington, DC, 1972.

O'Connell, Frances Hunt, *Giving and Growing*, St. Mary's Press, Winona, MN, 1990.

Cynthia Buser
St. Joseph School
Jefferson City, Missouri

Jeannine Fortunate
Our Lady of Mount Carmel School
Niagara Falls, New York

Stepping Stones to Staff Faith Development: The Principal as Facilitator

Journey of faith. Conversion. Change of heart. Process. These words are all too familiar and yet so significant when thinking about faith development. Faith development is a process. It is a journey from birth to death. When staff members reach our schools, they are somewhere on a faith continuum. Ministering in a Catholic school requires much more than academic credentials. It calls for an openness to the Spirit, a living faith, and a desire to deepen one's relationship with Christ. It is the principal who has the responsibility of discerning the needs of the staff and of designing ways of opening, deepening, searching, questioning the journey into faith. Buetow (1988) stated:

> The principal sets the spirit of the Catholic school, estab-
> lishes its patterns of discipline, and inspires in the school
> community a vision of what it can become. She or he is
> at once the exemplar and the facilitator. In the Catholic
> school, the principal cannot have doubts about the school's
> exact identity. It is the Christian vision that must orches-
> trate the whole. Principals, and other Catholic school ad-
> ministrators, must never lose a clear mental vision of Christ's
> face, or their heart's hearing of his word. (p. 259)

The Catholic school exists to ensure that the gospel of Jesus Christ is integrated into all aspects of living and learning. It is this purpose that distinguishes the Catholic school from other schools (National Conference of Catholic Bishops, 1972.) To fulfill the four-fold intent of Catholic education—to teach doctrine, to build community, to be of service, and to worship—the faith development of the staff must be given top priority.

From our experiences, we have found three ways that contribute to the faith development of staff members. The first is to provide a special library containing spiritual reading books, prayer books, cassette and video tapes, and magazines. See the Appendix for some selections to include in a school spiritual library.

Secondly, principals can design a school-wide faith development goal on a yearly basis. Listed below are some recommended books for a principal's use.

- Study Church related documents:
  To Teach as Jesus Did
  The Catholic School
  Lay Teachers in Schools: Witnesses to Faith
  The Religious Dimension of Education in a Catholic School
  Learning to Live as Jesus Did

- Use, as a two-year faith program, *Sharing the Faith: A Faculty Program for Catholic Schools* or the more brief *To Bring the Good News*, both from NCEA. Another similar resource is *Teachers, Catholic Schools, and Community: A Program of Spirituality.*

- View and discuss religious video or cassette tapes. A few staff members could take a common lunch time or break to enjoy and share together.

- Provide opportunities for prayer and liturgy. Certainly worship is an integral aspect of all our schools. Some helpful suggestions follow.

  - ✔ Principal's participation in the planning of school Masses and paraliturgies.
  - ✔ A once-a-week brief time to gather as a staff for prayer. An example would be to come together each Wednesday morning since it is mid-week. Any announcements could be given, questions could be asked, and a closing spiritual thought or reflection on the day's Mass readings could be shared. Following a moment of quiet prayer, more commonly known as centering prayer, one teacher commented that she "became so at peace and this was so easy to do."
  - ✔ Become comfortable with the "breaking open the Word process." Adults and children involved in the catechumenate stage of the RCIA throughout the world are enriched by the "breaking open the Word process" and its component called Lectionary-based catechesis. Specifically, the process leads one to see his or her life story being formed in "his or her heart's hearing of His

word" and being transformed into the living of the gospels in his or her daily life. Thus, if principals are nourished by the scriptures, surely staff members will likewise be empowered by the Word of God.

✔ Plan for a day of recollection. Innumerable resources are available. Staffs who have delved deeper into the spirituality of the Myers-Briggs and the Enneagram soon realize how human everyone is and how God truly loves us unconditionally.

✔ The numerous parables found in the writings of Edward Hays, John Shea, Gene Edwards, and others can also become means for spiritual reflection and sharing. Hays' book *St. George and the Dragon* offers a parable on the Our Father. One quote from this parable that lends itself to staff reflection and sharing reads: "Once you know these things, not with your head but with your heart, you can read any book and it will be a holy book. You can sing any song and it will be a sacred song. For when you are true to your special word, what Jesus said will be true in your life—that he and the Father will come and make their dwelling place with you, always!" (p. 95)

A third way for principals to provide a faith formation is to suggest that staff members set a yearly personal spiritual goal as part of their professional development plan. Some specifics to accomplish this may be helpful.

- Encourage the staff to listen to cassette tapes on various faith development topics as they drive to school or relax in some corner in their home.
- Encourage the staff to read spiritual books and magazines. One book a year is a manageable goal. Leave Catholic magazines or brief inspirational leaflets in the staff restrooms as well as in the lounge.
- Encourage the staff to attend workshops and lectures sponsored by the local parish, parishes, or diocese. (Remember to budget for staff faith development.)
- Continue to see "Christ's face" (Buetow) in each another. The small but so important ways that principals show concern and give support to staff members are the very ways that they in turn will reach out to one another and to the children and students. Examples include dropping a card or note with a word of praise, encouragement, or compassion, stopping to

listen to the personal joys and sorrows, sending food or other items to the member's family that is celebrating an event or is grieving a death. These few suggestions seem to be so commonplace and taken for granted; however, they and the many other ideas become the lived faith for each other.

It is hoped that the above recommendations will enhance the already present faith community in Catholic schools. Buetow states clearly that the principal "inspires in the school community a vision of what it can become." And when that faith community is believed and felt among all the staff members, then the students and families likewise will experience and know the same living faith. In acknowledging that community, any number of parents have written words similar to this parent's feelings.

> The atmosphere at St. N's for the students to learn and grow, not only in the field of academics, but also in the broader spectrum of human relationships is wonderful. The religious education will give them a foundation in their faith that is so important in the world we live in today. I wish all of you the best in your endeavors to keep the traditions of Catholic education alive and moving forward. (Patricia Grabber, letter of July 22, 1991)

Resources

Buetow, Harold A., *The Catholic School: Its Roots, Identity, and Future,* Crossroads, New York, 1988.

Congregation for Catholic Education, *The Catholic School,* Daughters of St. Paul, Boston, MA, 1977.

Congregation for Catholic Education, *The Religious Dimension of Education in a Catholic School,* United States Catholic Conference Publishing Services, Washington, DC, 1988.

Convey, F.S.C., Kevin and Wojcicki, Fr. Ted, *Teachers, Catholic Schools, and Faith Community: A Program of Spirituality,* Le Jacq Publishing, Inc., 1982.

Hays, Edward, *St. George and the Dragon,* Forest of Peace Books, Inc., Easton, KS, 1987.

Learning to Live as Jesus Did, Diocese of Amarillo, TX, 1992.

National Conference of Catholic Bishops, *To Teach as Jesus Did,* Washington, DC, United States Catholic Conference, 1972.

Sacred Congregation for Catholic Education, *Lay Teachers in Schools: Witness to Faith,* Boston, MA, Daughters of St. Paul, 1987.

Sharing the Faith: A Faculty Program for Catholic Schools, Washington, DC, National Catholic Educational Association, 1992.

Walsh, C.S.J., Maria Joseph, *To Bring the Good News*, Washington, DC, National Catholic Educational Association, 1992.

Books

Bernier, SSS, Paul, *Bread Broken and Shared*, Ave Maria Press, IN, 1981.

Doohan, Leonard, *Leisure: A Spiritual Need*, Ave Maria Press, IN, 1990.

Farrel, Edward, J., *Gathering The Fragments*, Ave Maria Press, IN, 1987.

Gavigan, Patricia Beall, *Journey Into God*, Ave Maria Press, IN, 1991.

Grana, Janice, *Images of Women in Transition*, St. Mary's Press, MN, 1991.

Gula SS, Richard M., *To Walk Together Again*, Paulist Press, NY, 1984.

Hofinger, Johannes, SJ, *Prayer Services for the Christian Educator*, NCEA, Washington, DC, 1983.

O'Malley, William J., *Daily Prayers for Busy People*, St. Mary's Press, MN, 1990.

Ripple, Paula, *Growing Strong at Broken Places, Ave Maria Press, IN, 1986.*

Rohr, Richard, *Simplicity: The Art of Living*, Crossroads Publications, NY, 1991.

Stenerson, Ruth, *Bible Readings For Teachers*, Augsburg Publishing House, MN, 1982.

Walsh, Maria Joseph,CSJ, *Inviting the Faculty to Prayer: A Practical Packet*, NCEA, Washington, DC, 1986.

Wiederkehr, Macrina,OSB, *Seasons of Your Heart,* HarperCollins, CA, 1985.

Magazines

Bible Today
Catechist
Living Faith
Praying
Religion Journal
Today's Catholic Teacher

Tapes

Anthony, OFM, Edd., *Reflections on the Serenity Prayer*, Franciscan Canticle, CA, 1992.

Barrett, S.S., Stephen, *Where is God When I'm Hurting?*, Ave Maria Press, IN, 1987.

Binns, Emily, *Who is Christ For Us Today?*, Ave Maria Press, IN, 1987.

Breault, S.J., William, *Wellsprings of Prayer*, Ave Maria Press, IN, 1988.

Cavanagh, Michael, *A Gift of Ministry*, Ave Maria Press, IN, 1988.

Groome, Thomas, *The Heart of Catholic Education*, Credence Cassettes, MO, 1986.

Johnson, Anne, *Stress and Spirituality*, Ave Maria Press, IN, 1986.

Kelly, Maureen, *Developing a Mature Conscience*, Credence Cassettes, MO, 1987.

Livingston, Patricia, *Learning From Life*, Ave Maria Press, IN, 1988.

Mergenhagen, John, *Prayer From the Heart*, Credence Cassettes, MO, 1988.

Murphy, Roland E., *Psalms as Prayer*, Ave Maria Press, IN, 1987.

Nouwen, Henri, J.M., *Who Are We?*, Ave Maria Press, IN, 1992.

Ripple, Paula, *Promises of the Rainbow*, Ave Maria Press, IN, 1986.

Ripple, Paula, *When Relationships End*, Ave Maria Press, IN, 1992.

Videos

O'Malley, OFM, Cap., Bishop Sean, *Reflections on Prayer*, Daughters of St. Paul, MA, 1987.

Pennington, Basil, *A Matter of Love*, Credence Cassettes, MO.

Rohr, Richard, *The Four Gospels*, Credence Cassettes, MO, 1989.

Davlyn Duesterhaus
St. Mary's School
Amarillo, TX

Margaret C. Purcell, Ed.D
Immaculate Heart of Mary School
Belmont, CA

Be My Rainbow in this Place: The Principal and Social Justice Issues in the Catholic Elementary School

B e my rainbow in this place
Signalling hope,
Signalling mercy,
Signalling my never failing promises.
Be my rainbow spanning the divide,
Bridging the gap,
Linking this place to heaven.
Be my rainbow
My life shining through
Shielding light in the darkness,
Heralding a new beginning.

Hazel Dickson's poem, quoted above, will never find its way into an anthology of major poets, but written as it was, against the backdrop of civil unrest in war-torn Belfast, it speaks volumes to me, as principal, as citizen, as Catholic.

In Northern Ireland there are many Church systems, and generations have been taught the "Catholic" way, the "Church of Ireland" way or the "Presbyterian" way etc., but education toward social issues was not part of the program. We learned the Corporal and Spiritual Works of Mercy, but we applied them to "our own." And when we were taught to "reach out," it was to the "pagan" in far-off lands. When we reflected on social conditions, it was on how they affected "our crowd," not giving heed to the reality that some of the "other crowd" had the same problems. Now, many years later, that system of separateness is being called into question and I, a product of that excellent educational system, which in the main, seems to have failed the basic test of recognizing and respecting Christ in all peoples, feel compelled to write of social issues in the Catholic school system. I feel compelled, because I do not believe it was the separateness of the schools as much as the politicizing of religion which caused the breakdown in Northern Ireland. While being political, I feel it is a drawback to become partisan. If ever there was a rainbow stance, this is it. As principal, I must span the issues, but not become embroiled in political jargon.

The rainbow has two ends. The pot of gold on one end is the Scripture, replete with the urgings of the prophets. The pot of gold at the other end is the goodness of God reflected in all creation. I must constantly dip into both.

Social justice defined

When I posed to staff the question of how I, as principal, might address social justice in the organization of the school, school policies, among staff and students, they invariably responded with, "Just exactly what do you mean by 'social justice?'" In this paper "social justice" is the fleshing out of the scriptural mandate to "do unto others as you would have them do unto you." It includes the concept of being our "brother's keeper" and of recognizing the common bond between men and women of all times and places. As Dietrich Bonhoeffer points out, "Christian brotherhood is not an ideal which we must realize: it is rather a reality created by God in Christ in which we may participate." From this point of view, social justice is a gift from God, by which I recognize the need to be informed about all human beings and to be sufficiently caring to make sure that the common good of all is addressed as adequately as possible. If then, I, as principal of a Catholic school am to be truly a leader, I have an obligation to make the gift come alive, to be the irridescent rainbow, reflecting light in the darkness.

Social justice demands accessibility

In her article, "Privilege, Education and Responsibility," in *The Educational Forum* (Winter, 1993) Judith Wheeldon asks an audacious question:

> Private schools, other than those conducted by religious institutions for nonaffluent pupils or that are established for some charitable purpose, do not face an easy task in justifying their existence as privileged institutions in otherwise, at least nominally, egalitarian societies. How can we justify the money and other resources spent on our students when so many have so little?

This challenging viewpoint is held by many Catholics who cannot "afford" Catholic education for their children, as well as by many parish finance councils who look on Catholic schools as a financial drain. In the organization of the school, I, as principal, am obliged to make sure that the school is indeed not a haven for the affluent or those who merely seek refuge from what they perceive to be a less than perfect public system. That means that the call for solvency must not be so rigid as to eliminate the concept of tuition assistance. I, the principal, as executive officer of the school commission ensure that an endowment is put in place and that development, conjointly advocated by the parish and school, is a top priority. In this way, conviction of the value of the mission, is seen in the "future" approach and fiscal responsibility is addressed.

Social justice demands fairness in distribution

Availability to all does not mean largesse. It means calling all to assume proportionate responsibility. In *Octogesima Adveniens*, Pope Paul VI alerts us to the tendency to expect others to rectify the injustices of the world when he points out that:

> It is easy to throw back on others the responsibility for injustices, if at the same time one does not realize how each one shares in it personally and how personal conversion is needed first. This basic humility will rid action of all inflexibility and sectarianism; it will also avoid discouragement in the face of a task which seems limitless in size.

I have come to believe that tuition assistance means the education of parents in consciousness of the limited resources of the needs of others and the need to assess and prioritize spending during their children's school years. This is not an easy task. I identify five essential elements needed in our tuition assistance program. These are:

a. establishment of need through a standardized procedure
b. a determination of financial ceiling for reception of assistance
c. close scrutiny of all extenuating circumstances which would have bearing on "a" and "b"
d. a willingness to re-evaluate upon appeal
e. a willingness to seek out other resources when demand exceeds budgeted amount.

As principal, I am willing to give of my time, my creativity and encouragement, but in that process I involve our tutition assistance committee made up of a representative of the school commission and two other parents. This is a shared responsibility, not a unilateral decision on the apportionment of community wealth.

The power of education in the struggle for social justice

Over and over again, in *Rerum Novarum, Quadragesimo Anno, Populorum Progressio* and *Octogesima Adveniens*, the popes have exhorted the faithful to be aware of, and to make use of the power of education in its ability to change the fortunes of humanity. In *Populorum Progressio*, Paul VI puts it very succinctly when he says, "Educators, it is to be your resolution and decision to instill in youth a love for people oppressed by poverty."

Our students are more prone to recognize ownership of the good climate of the school when the student council is seen as important and its members are given opportunity to lead in all aspects of school and to be innovative. Nor need leadership be confined to the student council. Even the youngest grouping can be given responsibility for making their school a better place. As I write, I have in mind the leadership of a group of first grade students, who gave up some time after school to weed out and prepare to plant seeds in a patch of ground around the front of the school building. They researched their project so that the plants would survive the summer heat without watering. This may seem a far cry from social justice. But is it? Is it not just to listen to, and affirm the goodness in all, and to allow each person to grow in his own self-worth. As pointed out in Goal 4 of the document "Catholic Schools of Western Washington," in a quote from *Gravissimum Educationis* ("Declaration on Christian Education" October 28, 1965) "Catholic schools...are no less zealous than other schools in the promotion of culture and in the formation of young people...the Catholic school prepares its students to contribute effectively to the welfare of the poor of the world."

Social justice reflected in the curriculum

Where the power of education is really seen and where the call to be rainbow is most obvious is in the religion and social studies programs, especially in the upper and middle grades. As principal, I need to be involved, available and encouraging, seeking every opportunity to keep alive the issues of social justice while not permitting the students to be either brain-washed or indoctrinated by use of negative criticism of the opposition. Current events discussed from all angles, without requiring that the students subscribe to the ideas of the teacher are excellent avenues of awakening the minds of the students. This was brought home when the United States entered the Gulf War. For those students whose relatives were fighting, the war was inevitable. For others, it was something which should have been avoided. The answer was to discuss the nature of war, the so-called "just war," the necessity or non-necessity of war. Then that was placed opposite the teachings of the Church and of Christ, and students were encouraged to come to their own conclusions, since in this instance, even the Church seems to have a checkered response to war.

In our quest for social justice, Raymond Raynes of the Community of the Resurrection, writing in 1943 and as quoted by Cecil Kerr pointed out:

> There is a grave danger, in the face of the appalling social disorder and injustices of our time, of imagining that we can produce some kind of a new order which is called Christian, and having forced it upon society by legislation or revolution, consider that we have planted firm foundations upon which will arise a temple of the Holy Spirit. This is an idle dream because it overlooks the fundamental fact that the heart of all our problems is the heart of man.

The admonition was true in 1943 and it remains true in 1993, and as true within a school as within the wider community. Here is precisely what I meant when I referred to the various church schools of Northern Ireland. We failed to recognize the fault and obligation within and refused to reach out to the "other."

Current events must not always be seen in the spectacular. Teachers of the junior high level do well to alert their students to the judicial system by observation of the courts in session, to the political system by listening to and analyzing the speeches and actions of paid politicians of city, state, and national government, and by analyzing city and state laws and judging their efficacy. But all this can only come about through the encouragement of the teachers by the principal. I, as principal, have an obligation to monitor the productivity of such programs.

Social justice and the staff of the Catholic school

Finally, I maintain that the quality of the school is in direct proportion to the value placed by the principal upon the spiritual, economic, and social support of the staff. I make sure that staff have an opportunity at the beginning of the school year, at Advent, Lent, and at the end of the school year to set aside a time for spiritual renewal as a group. All support staff, including custodian and secretary are a part of this important faith dimension. At certain points within the year, time is taken for a lunch or a dinner together, sometimes the base is broadened to include pastoral council and school commission.

I have consistently been an advocate for a concerted effort toward just salaries and benefits for all staff. Difficult as this has been at times, it is the one area where I concretely make known my appreciation of the sacrifices the staff make to remain faithful to Catholic education and the mission of our school. The hard part in adhering to social justice is the need to counsel a staff member to seek employment elsewhere. Here the call to be "rainbow shedding light in darkness" is at work. I find it necessary to protect both teacher and students and lead both to a new beginning. It is the toughest application of social justice. But I find strength in the words of Catherine de Hueck Doherty:

> ...to act according to God's will, one must empty oneself of all self-centeredness, selfishness, egotism. Positively one must have a listening heart that is free, poor, one that listens to the quiet voice of God and follows it.

I do not always find it easy to be an advocate of social justice within the school setting. Often the most obvious applications pass me by, but the prophet Micah provides my measuring rod when he proclaims,

" ....what does the Lord require of you, but to act justly, to love mercy, and walk humbly with your God?"

The rainbow is a sign of the humility of God. I accept God's invitation:

"Be my rainbow in this place."

Resources

Bonhoeffer, Deitrich, *Life Together* (SCM 1954), p. 18.

Caird, G. B., "Gospel of Luke," Pelican Gospel commentary, Penguin, 1971, p. 104.

Dicken, Susan J., "Ethnic Irrelevance & The Immigrant: Finding a Place For Minority Language," *The Educational Forum*, Vol. 57 #2, Winter, 1993, Kappa Delta Pi, West Lafayette, IN, pp. 120-125.

Dickson, Hazel, "Be My Rainbow," Founder of Members of Cornerstone Community, Belfast.

deHueck-Doherty, Catherine, T*he Gospel Without Compromise*, Ave Maria Press, Notre Dame, IN, 1976.

Imber, Michael & Schewack, James Joseph, "Educational Reforms Can Produce Societal Inequities: A Case Study," *Educational Administrative Quarterly*, Vol. 27 #3, August, 1991.

Kerr, Cecil, *The Way of Peace: Peace Amidst the Conflict in Northern Ireland*, Hodder & Stoughton, London, Sydney, Auckland, Toronto, 1990.

McInnis et al., *Educating For Peace & Justice: Religious Dimensions*, Institute For Peace & Justice, St. Louis, MO, 1984.

Pope Paul VI, *Gravissimum educationis*, 10/28/65, *Octogesima Adveniens, Social Problems*, 5/15/71, *Populorum Progressio*, 1967.

Sarasson, S.B., *The Culture of the School and The Problem of Change*, Boston, Allyn and Bacon, 1982.

Sister Angela McCarthy
Immaculate Conception School
Mount Vernon, Washington

Weaving a Value System throughout a School Curriculum

Imagine a tall stairway without a railing. Imagine a room without a window or flowing air system. Imagine a car radio without speakers. That is what a Catholic school is like without an integrated religion curriculum. A bannister by itself is not too helpful. A room without a cooling system is stuffy. It has no fresh air. A radio without speakers is limited in its use.

How rich it would be to have religion running constantly and consistently throughout the curriculum! This means for me that religion is not simply the message we relay during our specific religion class but our modelling as each day unfolds.

In reflecting over my current and my previous school experiences, I have found that Christian values can be enfleshed in all areas of our curriculum. I believe this begins primarily with a staff that prays together and is serious about their relationship with God. If we can lead our teachers to prayer, to journalling, to a spiritual journey, I believe that they will want to integrate values or religious ideas and vision with all their subjects. I have found that monthly faculty meetings are a ripe time to begin spiritual reflection. By a reading or song, reflection can begin. Journalling and/or sharing encourages those who want to share insights or reflections. As the year progresses, you will find more teachers becoming ready and able to share themselves and their values. I have found that the teachers look forward to this "quiet time" and it has proved beneficial in setting and grounding our Catholic identity.

Another way I have found religion to be coordinated as a thread through all our programs has been through social outreach projects. These projects may originally start out as a simple project but if done strategically they can add meat to a subject. To be effective, I feel they must move from a single action to fostering an attitude. Some concrete examples follow.

Our primary classes and their teachers have adopted babies from the Right to Life Center in our local town. Initially the class had a bake sale to raise funds so they could go shopping to buy gifts for foster babies or unwanted babies. What began as a "Christmas project" has led to a further discussion of abortion, adoption, and respect for all forms of life. Through this social action the value of life has been explored in many aspects through health, through science, and through social studies. It has expanded into English as letters are shared with mothers-to-be in a local home for unwed mothers.

Our liturgies both at school or on Sundays have begun to show our children respect for the word of God as well as acceptance of themselves as participants in a celebration. I feel that their proclamation of the readings has influenced them in a way that touches many aspects of their day, whether at recess or in dealing with a difficult classmate. Of course, it is not going to make life peaceful or perfect. I have had occasions where specific readings have entered into class meetings or classroom discussions.

Our school works with the Holy Childhood Association each year by contributing money to their cause and by integrating the values of children from other lands into our curriculum. This program enables us to learn about and absorb a little of their cultures into our Social Studies curriculum. This has helped us form our values in regard to respect for all people in our world.

Another worthwhile attitude-building project is that of having foreign exchange students as part of our school family. Again, we have found that this cultural exchange strengthens our values of respecting other cultures. The effect of sharing with the students has lasted long after they have returned to their homelands.

The strategic long range planning project that our school is currently involved in with a professional company has been an invaluable value-building process. As this representative group of teachers, school board members, parents, local business personnel, and public school educators meet and share, we continue to enflesh our values and discuss how they can be incorporated into our curriculum. We are just beginning this project and look forward to moving through it. It has proven to be an excellent binding, clarifying, and strengthening process for all involved both to see what our values are and how we will support and promote them.

Our daily prayer together as a school community has been influential also in this regard. *Children's Daily Prayer* by Elizabeth Jeep is a wonderful resource to use. It is set up liturgically according to the season or the feast of the day. Often the introduction, the psalms, and the readings can be used in other subject areas for discussion. This is a very practical way to integrate religion into other subjects in the curriculum. Studying the origins of feasts or customs has led to some interesting and worthwhile research and discussion in English or

Social Studies classes.

Another useful experience in helping teachers to weave religion and the study of values throughout the curriculum has been re-evaluating and rewriting the school's mission statement. In the process of reflecting on and stating what our mission is, we have come to set our priorities to proclaim who we are as educators, who we are serving and what our motivating force is. As we shared our reflections and beliefs, I feel as a community we began to respect each other on a deeper level and became more committed to our students and to this particular Catholic school. We are becoming more attuned to the differing needs of our various students. I feel writing the mission statement has been a strong building block in strengthening the Catholic identity in our school and has helped us to stretch our values throughout the curriculum. Two excellent resources to use before beginning a mission statement project are the videos, *The Power of Vision* by Stephen Barkley and *Principal Centered Leadership* by Stephen Covey. They both speak of the process of identifying and buying into a value system.

I believe that if we as staff are clear as to what our values are and we believe that these are the values that we want to share with our students, we will begin to see and feel that these same values are enriched, spoken, and modelled throughout our curriculum and in every aspect of our school. As Steven Barkley stated so clearly in this video, *The Power of Vision,* "If we grab the rope, we are ready for the plunge of tomorrow." I see that if we are ready to accept the challenge of incorporating values into our curriculum and we work deliberately at this task, we will make a difference and help ourselves and our children hold onto our values as tomorrow comes. I see this statement saying that if we are the chlorine in a pool of moving water, if we are the clarifying, purifying agent in our schools, the values we share can help put a focus on how we set our days, in which direction we move and how we share our vision with the children so as to weave together an integrated meaningful curriculum, one that speaks of our values as Christian educators. It is possible and we can do it.

Resources

Barkley, Stephen, *The Power of Vision*
Covey, Stephen, *Principal Centered Leadership*
Jeep, Elizabeth, *Children's Daily Prayer*, Liturgical Press, 1992.

Sister Rosemary Fonck
Sacred Heart School
Effingham, Illinois

Section V
Diversity

Gender Discrimination in the Catholic Elementary School Classroom

I f, historically, the majority of Catholic school principals, and teachers have been women, why is gender discrimination present in Catholic school classrooms? Research might indicate the following: church male domination over women religious principals, societal stereotyping of both men and women and educational resources.

This type of research might be interesting, but not effective in reducing the gender discrimination that exists in the elementary classroom, including the Catholic school elementary classroom. What I will explore in this reflection will be helpful to myself and hopefully to other Catholic school principals: How can I assist the teachers in my school to be aware of gender discrimination in their classrooms? How can I work with teachers to be sensitive to every student in the classroom, regardless of gender?

Recently, I reflected on my own development and became aware of gender discrimination in my own educational process. Discussing this with current faculty members and teacher applicants, I discovered that they had experienced discrimination in their lives. In reality, my colleagues and I could be included in the statistics for the review literature offered in the references of this paper.

As an elementary school child and as a high school student, (I attended a public elementary school and a Catholic high school) I never received affirmation for almost perfect scores in mathematics nor for my interest in science. Yet, I spent almost all of my spare time practicing my handwriting which I never mastered (I now only use the keyboard) and studying spelling. (Spell check was designed for me.) Statistically, I qualify for Dolores A. Grayson's research which states, "Generally, males are given feedback directly to the task, content or thought process involved. More often than not, females are given feedback related to the appearance of their work. Appearance is a dominant influence related to females in many aspects of their lives." (Grayson, p. 7) As a teacher of math in grades seven and eight for nineteen years, I regretfully testify that I modeled the same type of discrimination I experienced in elementary school. Many men who were once my seventh and eight grade math students are accountants, engineers, or in some math/science related profession. To my knowledge, only one woman I taught is a math teacher.

As recently as this spring, I evaluated and interviewed the youngest teacher on the faculty in which I serve as principal. This teacher began her career at school three years ago. This very outstanding and promising educator is an English major who, as often still happens, was assigned to teach Science and Computers in fifth through eighth grades. She did this extremely successfully for two years. Currently she teaches Language Arts to seventh and eighth grades. As her principal, I rated her as an outstanding science teacher. Her enthusiasm about the subject matter excited the students. This excitement was reflected in the students' success in the subject and their enthusiasm about their science activities. Why, I asked, had she not majored in an area of science? "Oh," she replied, "I always loved science and algebra, and was good at it, too, but I needed to let my brother succeed. He had failed a grade so he was in my class. Teachers really encouraged him and always told him he could succeed. I understood everything and really knew my algebra, but I just kept quiet." (This teacher attended a Catholic elementary school and a public high schoool.) Succeed her brother did. He received a scholarship to Annapolis for engineering." Effort statements are used more frequently with males, than with females. With females, the emphasis is frequently limited to whether they have exerted any effort at all." (Grayson, p. 7) This young teacher continued to say, "You know, I behave the same way my teachers behaved. I always pay more attention to the boys; they demand it, you know. Next year, though, I am paying more attention to the quiet girls. They are such solid students, and I never spend time with them. I don't even know them."

Based on experiences of school gender discrimination both in my personal and professional life as well as a review of literature about classroom gender discrimination, I suggest that we integrate into the regular classroom observation forms a checklist to assess teacher appoach in reference to gender. Personally, I hope that this addition into classroom observation forms encourages a new teacher awareness of how to make our Catholic school more Christian in its approach to every child, male and female.

I make this suggestion with an awareness that boys, too, have been discriminated against in other ways. "For instance, it is generally assumed that compassion, kindness, passivity, and patience are feminine traits. In opposition to that aggression, independence, vulgarity, and competitiveness are considered male traits." (Glickman, p., 6) It is my opinion that the various family life programs (the MacMillan *Fully Alive* series and the Benziger *Family Life* program) used in our Catholic schools have successfully begun to eliminate the stereotyping of boys as persons who are not capable of expressing feelings of compassion and care. The family life programs have also brought sensitivity to teachers and helped them to understand that many male traits have been taught or imposed on small boys and are not part of their nature. However, despite the problems experienced by boys, it seems that the need to eliminate the academic stereotyping of girls demands our greater attention.

The observation checklist I propose is a gleaning of ideas from personal experience and from the review of the literature listed in the references of this article.

SENSITIVE TO GENDER DISCRIMINATION
Classroom observation checklist

Curriculum. "Some of the most persistent obstacles to equitable career choices, college study and employment are the subject areas of math, science, and computer learning. As females move into adolescence, their interest in science usually wants and their achievement lags behind that of males. It is not uncommon for gifted adolescent females to repress their academic abilities or opt out of advanced math and science to avoid risking their grade point average. The role of mathematician or scientist is perceived as masculine, although many of these same females will choose careers which require math or science skills. They later regret their decisions and/or lack of encouragement." (Grayson, pp. 11-12)
- ❑ Evidence that every student is afforded an opportunity to activities in every curricular area.

Physical environment.
- ❑ Evidence that seating arrangement is not gender discriminating.
- ❑ Evidence that bulletin board displays are inclusive.

Teaching style, method, approach. The problem with traditional pedagogy is that it rewards learning that is associated with rational, objective approaches and, as it happens, with male students. Frequently, the mark of success becomes the grade that a student achieves rather than the student's development of the ability to make meaning, especially in the case of women and minority students. (Her & Tetreault, p. 58) "For girls, 'I win, you lose' is a problematic stance, since it is since it is potentially divisive and threatens connections between group members." (Shakeshaft, p. 3)

- ❑ Evidence of collaborative/cooperative learning.
- ❑ Evidence that competition is not the sole motivation.
- ❑ Evidence of connecting learning to experience.
- ❑ Evidence of various approaches other than lectures.
- ❑ Evidence of class discussion.
- ❑ Evidence of inclusive language.

Questions. Studies generally seem to suggest that males are given more opportunities to respond to higher level questions. "If a teacher falls into habit of asking simple recall questions of some students and reserving the higher-level questions for a select group of students, an inequitable situation exists. Some students are receiving a lower quality of instruction than other students." (Grayson, p. 11)

- ❑ Opened ❑ Closed ❑ Directed toward all students.
- ❑ Answers analyzed (how and for whom)
- ❑ Answers affirmed (how and for whom)
- ❑ Answers acknowledged (how)
- ❑ Abstract
- ❑ Experiential

Responses. "Teachers are less inclined to encourage females to risk or expand a response. If the teacher always accepts a student's 'I don't know' or nonresponse without probing, that student learns to avoid risking a response. Females are taught to be listeners and males are encouraged to speak. Consequently, females generally have more difficulty than males in getting attention when they wish to say something. This process circles back to denigrate the importance of what females say. Males have been less motivated to develop listening skills which is a limitation in interpersonal relations." (Grayson, pp. 9-10)

- ❑ Opportunity to respond (Who responds?)
- ❑ Type of feedback (Who is allowed to think? How much time is given to think before answering? Who is given more time?)
- ❑ Physical approach (Where is the teacher standing in relation to students who are given the opportunity to respond?)
- ❑ Criticism of response (Which students are guided to correct answers? Which students are told answers are wrong and left without assistance to conclude the correct answer?)
- ❑ Type of responses (To whom and in what way? Single word responses? Nods? Elaborations?)

Opportunities for Self-Expression. "Teachers allow more opportunities for boys to respond — to answer questions, engage in activities, give opinions, help out, etc. . The average female is ignored — neither reprimanded nor praised. The high-achieving female receives the least attention of all students. Both majority and minority girls learn that their opinions are not valued, that their responses to questions are not worthy of attention. Consequently, female students come to believe that they are not smart or important." (Shakeshaft, p. 4)
- ❑ Facts
- ❑ Feelings
- ❑ Opinions
- ❑ Assertiveness

Evaluation/Assessment. "Considerable evidence suggests that our views of females as good with words and males as good with numbers affects both how we evaluate their learning and what they actually learn." (Grayson, p. 6)
- ❑ Written tests
- ❑ Oral tests
- ❑ Portfolios
- ❑ Competitive (grades and honor roll)

Activities. "An examination of the use of competition as a learning style provides an illustration of the ways in which male development guides instructional style....For girls, 'I win, you lose' is a problematic stance, since it is potentially divisive and threatens connections between group members." (Shakeshaft p. 1)
- ❑ Contests relational (i.e. tutorial, group)
- ❑ Cooperative/collaborative
- ❑ Individual

Environment
- ❑ Free of abusive sexist language (verbal, written, symbol).

This observation form or one similar will open an opportunity for principals to assess whether gender discrimination is present in the elementary school classroom.

References

Glickman, Jill M., "Social Studies for Preschool Children Through Cognitive Intervention of the Acquisition of Sex Role Stereotypes," *M.S. Practical*, Nova University, June, 1992.

Grayson, Dolores A., "Classroom and Site-Based Leadership Development: Increasing Achievement and Participation For All Students With An Emphasis on Underserved Populations," Paper presented to The American Education Research Association, San Francisco, April 20-24, 1992.

Maher, Frances and Tetreault, Mary K.T., "Inside Feminist Classrooms: An Ethnographic Approach," *New Directions For Teaching and Learning*, N. 49, Spring, 1992.

Shakeshaft, Charol, "A Gender At Risk," *Phi Delta Kappan*, Vol. 67, 1986.

Sister Carol Marie Wiatrek, CSSF
St. Joseph Elementary School
Pomona, California

Goodbye, Melting Pot!

Making my morning rounds one Monday in January, I was energized to see a variety of colorful projects in process. Many classes were preparing for Catholic Schools Week and each had a piece of good news. A flash of inspiration sent me back to the office for the handicam, so that these priceless moments could be captured on video.

My first stop was in a primary classroom. Jasmine and her group were drawing self-portraits for the Good News class quilt. I zoomed in on the box of crayons because I caught the debate between Pedelie and Sarah over what shade of brown or black was closest to the right skin color. Stopping by the locker room on my way to the intermediate wing my ears again perked up at a debate in Spanish or Portuguese. Popping my head in the door I asked Sergio and Pedro to keep the language universal.

As I approached the sixth grade I spotted Raymond directing the cooperative group in the rap practice. "We have Di-ver-si-tee...We have Un-i-tee..."

Saving the best until last, I found the school chapel buzzing with liturgy preparations. "Go forth, teach all nations" came from the student lector and budding artists were putting the final touches on the DIVERSITY+ UNITY=GOOD NEWS banners.

Yes, there are multicultural multi-ethnic activities in our school and efforts are being made to focus on our unity as well as diversity. As leaders in Catholic schools moving into the 21st century, how can we challenge people/staffs to:
- increase our multicultural/multi-ethnic appreciation
- become sensitive to the needs of our varied school population
- make adaptations within the school environment
- provide occasions to promote and encourage pride in ethnic diversity?

One of the first areas in the effort to expand appreciation would be offering staff updated knowledge, starting with clarifying terms. After a brief search, I found a number of clarifications for multicultural/multi-ethnic education. Macmillan McGraw-Hill has a book for educational publishing professionals, *Reflecting Diversity*. In it the authors refer to a study in the Detroit public schools that clarifies the new thinking on multiculturalism:

> Multicultural Multi-ethnic Education is an ongoing process that prepares people to value diversity and view cultural differences as a positive and vital force in the continued development of society. This process prepares people to live, learn and work in a pluralistic world. It promotes respect for the intrinsic worth of each individual regardless of ethnicity, race, religion, sex, socioeconomic, physical or mental condition and must be an essential part of the educational process.

Joseph Banks at the University of Washington, Seattle has a number of good books on multi-ethnic education. In multi-ethnic education he states that, "We can define an ethnic group as a group that shares a common ancestry, culture, history, tradition and sense of peoplehood." He goes on to clarify, "Multi-ethnic education is concerned with modifying the total school environment so that it is more reflective of the ethnic diversity within a society."

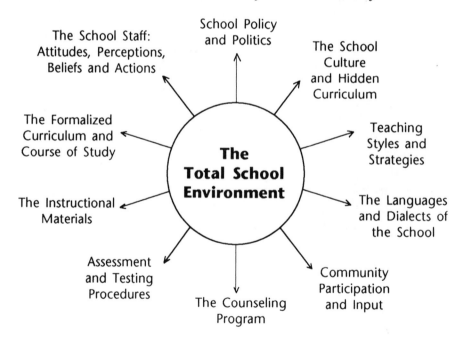

Figure 3.4. The Total School Environment—In this figure, the total school environment is conceptualized as a system that consists of a number of major identifiable variables and factors, such as the school culture, school policy and politics, and the formalized curriculum and course study. In the idealized multi-ethnic school, each variable reflects ethnic pluralism. Even though any one factor may be the focus of initial school reform, changes must take place in each factor in order to create and sustain an effective multi-ethnic educational environment.

This diagram is very helpful. It gives some framework to the topic and gives direction for goal setting. This is a tool that would be invaluable for planning with staff, parents, and boards.

Another tool for the principals to use is a "Criteria for Content Checklist" which could be used in the regular classroom evaluations. The Detroit public schools prepared *A Criteria for Content and Other Learning Materials Appropriate for Use in The Detroit Public Schools*. These criteria are valuable for a checklist for many areas of the school program:

Criteria and learning material for multicultural education

BALANCE—Infused with the concepts underlying multiculturalism such as the oneness of humanity and interdependence and interrelatedness of cultural and ethnic groups.

Are content and learning materials

- free of excesses /extremes/exaggerations/incomplete thoughts/ half truths?
- reflective of different viewpoints that encourage and foster critical thinking?
- diverse with instructional strategies?
- contextually balanced with regard to illustrations and portrayals of various cultural and ethnic groups?

HARMONY—Content and learning materials will be screened for harmony in these ways:

- words, names used should be the same as those used by the subject groups, i.e., call people what they call themselves.
- materials should be studied from the perspective of the group being taught.
- inclusion of various perspectives and significant examples of folklore, customs, symbols, and practices related to all ethnic groups.

BIAS-FREE

- overpresentation
- no underpresentation
- no stereotyping
- no deliberate selectivity of learning materials
- no glossing over issues
- no deliberate isolation and fragmentation
- no discriminatory language

The final and perhaps the most critical area of concern responds to the call of the National Congress directional statement: "We will educate our staffs, students, parents to reject racism, sexism, and discrimination."

Collaboration Across Cultural/Racial Lines

Conversion for Multicultural Living

other cultures		
ethnocentrism		
awareness		
understanding		
acceptance/respect		
appreciation/valuing		
selective adoption		
multicultural collaboration		
celebration		

Types of Collaboration
1. Creating newness building upon the differences
2. Creating newness building upon similarities
3. Cultural synergy: innovation

The process for using this chart is simple. Each staff member is asked to reflect on the following questions and fill in the first column of the chart.

After shared reflection, the second column is then answered in light of the school community.

Conversion for multicultural living chart: a practical plan for staff development

These guide questions are to be used with the chart.
The following are Levels of Growth as indicated on the chart.
- Ethnocentrism—When did we first realize there were people other than "my group?" When did we first realize that we were not "on top?"

- Awareness—Who? Where? How many? What is the sociology of the area? How conscious are we of the people in our area?
- Understanding—Why are these people here? Who brought them here? What brought them here? What happened historically that attracted them to this place?
- Acceptance/respect—How have I embraced these people? Are they here to stay? How do we accept them in ways that are enhancing to humanity?
- Appreciation/valuing—What do they bring to us that we do not have in our own culture? What stories/myths/music/symbols of their culture make ours richer?
- Selection/adoption—How does the school reflect the culture? How does it set a tone for welcoming all cultures all year? What has the school done to institutionalize values?
- Multicultural collaboration—How can we, by our differences/similarities, create something new?

Celebration: How is a new culture being born?
Conversion for Multicultural Living Checklist
- Incorporate multicultural choices in liturgy and prayer i.e., music, readings, drama, design
- Present/promote saints, heroes, prophets, models from all cultures
- Exhibit multicultural work in the building i.e., art forms—paintings, poetry, photography, pottery, musical instruments
- Encourage staff to wear multicultural clothes and jewelry
- Vary the decor in the building reflecting multicultural designs and colors
- Post welcome signs and posters in a variety of languages
- Attend multicultural events and exhibits
- Seek out the services of adults of color i.e., doctors, dentists, instructors, guest speakers
- Help students identify inaccuracies
- Give the staff a multicultural quiz
- Encourage people to respond to stereotypes in music, literature, publications
- Circulate a multicultural article that is thought provoking

When these are evident in a place, it reflects sensitivity to multiculturalism. This third and final tool is reflective in nature and could be shared over a period of time. A faculty retreat day makes an ideal starting point. The process is rooted in the gospel message found in Galatians:

"All of you who have been baptized into Christ have clothed

yourselves with him. There does not exist among you Jew or Greek, slave or free, male or female." (Gal. 2:28) It gives impetus to the prayer of thankfulness that we are "from every nation and race, people and tongue." (Rev. 7:9)

Going back through the school with the handicam after months of multicultural awareness, I'm sure the sights and sounds will reflect many different cultures. Each reminds us that "Jesus was born in one cultural milieu, but, as the Christ, speaks in and to all cultural milieus."

Sister Christine Kiley
St. Raphael School
Bridgeport, Connecticut

The Multicultural Classroom: How Do We Bring Them Together?

Educators have long struggled with the issue of commonality in a school with many nationalities. Many authors have addressed multicultural curricula in the areas of both language and content. Suggestions for festivals, ethnic fairs, and teaching units abound, but what is the factor that brings the school to the point of affirming everyone? How do we learn to work and play together while enriching each other with our cultural heritage? The answer is found in the way we live the Gospel and how we show that we are truly catholic Catholics.

At Mount Carmel Academy on Chicago's north side, students find themselves in a warm, caring environment based on respect. The teachers build self-esteem and affirm each student as a child of God. They are modeling the gospel message and giving students the security they need to share themselves and their cultures with one another.

The journey the faculty took to arrive at this level of comfort in the learning environment took about four years. The components that were studied and developed include: staff development, discipline, curriculum, and individual affirmation.

Faculty self-study is an on-going process and not something done in a single faculty meeting or in-service day. In the first phase staff members were asked to consider who they are, where they came from, and where they have been along the way. By determining our own experiences and biases, we begin to see how we fit into the multicultural picture. We then inform and enrich each other and therefore increase our understanding of the students in our care.

Communication among the faculty is as important to the process as any of the other components. The faculty must work, play, and pray together in order to achieve a level of contact that models friendship. Children perceive very quickly that a happy faculty cares about one another and thrives on harmony.

The second phase of the journey has two parts. First, the curriculum must incorporate the study of various cultures and not reflect only mainstream views and perspectives. Mount Carmel teachers have integrated the curriculum whenever possible and this has made the infusion of multicultural themes relatively easy.

There are many excellent resources available to assist schools. *Creating a Curriculum That Works: A Guide to Outcomes-Centered Curriculum Decision Making* by Lorraine Ozar, is available through NCEA. Diocesan offices sometimes have guides available. For example, *Guide for the Writing of the Curriculum* may be obtained from the Office of Catholic Education, Archdiocese of Chicago.

The second part of phase two concerns discipline. Catholic schools are noted for their strict discipline policies and many parents choose Catholic schools for just that reason. In a setting where many nationalities are present, it is imperative that the discipline code is firm, fair, consistent, and caring. At Mount Carmel the staff worked hard to put together a code that met the needs of over 35 nationalities.

At Mount Carmel, the list of what was expected of the students was condensed into five rules. These rules stated that students must respect adults, respect fellow students, respect school property, be in uniform, and be on time. ("On time" includes turning in assignments and getting to classes promptly.) Each teacher generates classroom rules and consequences with the children in September. A list of rights and responsibilities is posted in the main hall for all to view for the year.

Step-by-step procedures regarding discipline problems are printed in the parent handbook along with all policies from the archdiocese and the parish. Every case is handled swiftly and fairly. Parents are always involved. Every child is treated gently but firmly so that there can be no question of bias or preferential treatment.

After two years of writing, implementing, and revising the discipline code, and composing an integrated, interdisciplinary curriculum, the faculty took on the enormous task of affirmation. How do we recognize all of the nationalities that may be represented in our schools? Do we celebrate Black History Month or Hispanic Week? What about the Croatians, Serbs, or Yugoslavian Muslims? Should the Indians, Pakistanis, and Philippinos be lumped in with the Chinese, Burmese, Japanese, and Koreans? What about our families that are interracial or multi-ethnic?

With the recognition that we could not possibly affirm all these nationalities, came the realization that the Mount Carmel faculty already were. By providing an atmosphere of discipline based on respect, by recognizing the dignity and worth of each child, by interweaving Christian values into all aspects of our program, the teachers were affirming each one of our students as a child of God.

As the children have become more and more comfortable in the

Mount Carmel learning environment, their cultural traits and customs have begun to emerge. The children function in an atmosphere of mutual respect and therefore find the sharing of their cultural backgrounds interesting and enriching. Teachers are challenged every day to maintain an atmosphere of caring and to provide experiences that are culturally based.

The Office of Catholic Education in the Archdiocese of Chicago provides every school opportunity to examine their Catholic identity. A consultant from the Office of Religious Education works with the faculty and parents. With an elementary school principal, the consultant conducts a visit to the school in order to observe and report on the principal, teachers, and students in light of their Catholic identity.

The report that Mount Carmel received affirmed the fact that all the planning and hard work was indeed working. The consultant found that the message of the Gospel was visible and that the faculty and students at Mount Carmel were living in an atmosphere of caring and respect based on the principles of justice and peace.

That was the moment that the faculty came to the realization that our Catholic identity was the commonality that we were looking for all along. The characteristics that bind all these nationalities together was right under our noses. We are a Catholic school.

Margaret Sue Jungers
Mount Carmel Academy
Chicago, Illinois

Where in the World is Multicultural Education in Your School?

S tudents are using the stimulating computer game, "Where in the World is Carmen San Diego?" They map and track adventures while gathering information in books, encyclopedias, and other available sources. Students achieve success and arrive at their destinations at different times in this game. When they arrive depends upon the choices they make and the information they gather.

This reminds me of how multiculturalism is infused in our schools. Multicultural education is everywhere. We cannot elude it. We cannot ignore its impact on our students if we wish to truly prepare them for their future. As Catholic educators, we are challenged by various approaches which enhance the learning of our students and by having to provide them with all the information in our curricula. And yet, with the immense amount of information we provide, are we teaching our students to be members of a global society?

The importance of multicultural education is evident in the research regarding the changes in student population. The "minority" students are becoming the majority in many schools. By 1995, 50% of the high school graduating classes of thirteen states will be comprised of 29% to 50% of minority students. Also, as America interacts with the world, global awareness and understanding of diverse cultures will continue to be important for economic reasons.

The following basic assumptions about multicultural education were prepared by Hilda Hernandez:

- It is increasingly important for political, social, educational, and economic reasons to recognize that the United States is a culturally diverse society.
- Multicultural education is for all students.
- Multicultural education is synonymous with effective teaching.
- Teaching is a cross-cultural encounter.
- The educational system has not served all students well.
- Multicultural education is synonymous with educational in-

novation and reform.
- Next to parents, teachers are the single most important factor in the lives of children.
- Classroom interaction between teachers and students constitutes the major part of the educational process for most students.

Robert J. Cottrol states, "Perhaps our most important contribution to the twenty-first century will be to demonstrate that people from different races, cultures, and ethnic backgrounds can live side by side, retain their uniqueness and, over time, form a new common culture. That has been the American story. It is a history that has much to tell the world. It must be told by American educators."

Many of the schools in larger cities deal with several languages and cultures within their school community. On the other hand, rural communities must teach their children about other cultures in order to broaden their understanding of the world. For example, in our school, Immaculate Conception in rural South Dakota, we have three African-American children, two Native American children, and the remaining students are of various Caucasian descent.

Some of the activities that we have engaged in to promote multiculturalism during the past year include
- celebrating Columbus Day and Native American Day simultaneously
- having an African-American professor in as a guest speaker
- preparing a multicultural play which involved our fifth and sixth graders
- preparing to welcome a Japanese exchange teacher for the next academic year.

The reason I continue to believe in the importance of multicultural education is that through some life experiences, I know that people live without understanding their neighbors or appreciating what various groups have contributed to our society. For example, the Native-American culture is not recognized for the many contributions it has made. For this reason, we participated in an exchange program. The Knights of Columbus sponsored an exchange of sixth grade students between our school and a tribal school located one hour away. Our students spent a day with them which included a friendship dance (Pow-Wow). The following month, the tribal students visited our school and experienced art, music, a tour of our church, and a basketball game. The students gained a true understanding and respect for one another. They formed friendships which we hope will continue.

We had another experience which was absolutely astounding to me. As stated earlier we had invited an African-American college professor who shared various personal stories about things that had happened to her and her family. I was amazed at how our children responded when she began her presentation by asking them if they knew any black people. My students just sat there looking around uncomfortably at our African-American children. Our children of African-American descent didn't even raise their hands. It was as if they needed permission to acknowledge or to discuss their cultural differences. Later, in relating to the children, our speaker had a little shadow. The 4th grade African-American child simply "lit up." He couldn't seem to get close enough to this woman. He identified with her completely and exuberantly.

I share these experiences with you because I know each school's population and background is unique. It certainly seems to me that we need to do more than food fairs and coloring paper dolls during Catholic Schools Week. We need to build and mold a climate of acceptance of one another. We need to understand who we are, who you are, and what we can be together.

As students sit in awe of speakers who have experienced another country, they can ask questions and dialogue. Later, they can research and report on various countries. Their self-concepts can grow while they experience and integrate what they have learned throughout the curriculum at all grade levels. Awareness and acceptance will be enhanced. As Lily Wong Filmore stated in an article:

> What children must learn are some fundamental attitudes and values concerning life in a multicultural, multilingual society. They must be taught, early in life, that they live in a world where people come from many different places and backgrounds, but they are more alike than they are different. They need to recognize that differences in looks, likes, beliefs, and behavior are neither good nor bad—they are just different.

Her philosophy certainly is in keeping with the gospel values that permeate the traditions, curriculum and environment of Catholic education.

Charlotte Higuchi has written and taught several multicultural units in her classroom. She states, "My goal for all my students— American born or not, minority or not—is to develop cross-cultural acceptance, to have them develop strategies to work through their own prejudices and to sustain their own dignity when they become the targets of prejudice." As we develop units and activities we should keep this in mind. We can even take this a step further and say that multicultural education can be an everyday experience.

As you begin your journey on the road to multicultural education, challenge yourself to think of these things:
- Multiculturalism is a walk toward a common humanity.
- Teach your students that they are part of a much larger world.
- Include parents in the process as resource and advisory people.
- Plan to in-service your staff with continued opportunities for dialogue.

Where in the world are we in multicultural education? As we teach with global issues in mind, influenced by our love for God and all of his people, we are addressing the very heart of the matter. We are like multicultural education itself in that we are becoming community. The following poem summarizes it very beautifully.

Our first task
in approaching
another people,
another culture,
another religion
is to take off our shoes
for the place we are approaching
is holy.
Else we may find ourselves
treading on another's dream.
More serious still,
we may forget...
that God was there
before our arrival.
-author unknown

Resources

Cottrol, Robert J., "America the Multicultural," *American Educator Magazine,* Winter, 1990.

Filmore, Lily Wong, "Educating Citizens for a Multicultural 21st Century," *Multicultural Education,* Summer, 1993, pp. 10-12.

Higuchi, Charlotte, "Understanding Must Begin With Us," *Educational Leadership,* Vol. 50, no. 8, May 83, pp 69-71.

Eskey, Kenneth, "Minority Students Becoming Majority in Schools, Survey Says," *Washington Times,* September 13, 1991.

Hernandez, Hilda, *Multicultural Education: A Teachers Guide to Content and Process,* Macmillian/McGraw Hill, 1989

Sandra J. McGeough
Immaculate Conception School
Watertown, South Dakota